SERVICE ANIMALS IN SCHOOLS

SPECIAL EDUCATION LAW, POLICY, AND PRACTICE

Series Editors
Mitchell L. Yell, PhD, University of South Carolina
David F. Bateman, PhD, Shippensburg University of Pennsylvania

The *Special Education Law, Policy, and Practice* series highlights current trends and legal issues in the education of students with disabilities. The books in this series link legal requirements with evidence-based instruction and highlight practical applications for working with students with disabilities. The titles in the *Special Education Law, Policy, and Practice* series are designed not only to be required textbooks for general education and special education preservice teacher education programs but are also designed for practicing teachers, education administrators, principals, school counselors, school psychologists, parents, and others interested in improving the lives of students with disabilities. The *Special Education Law, Policy, and Practice* series is committed to research-based practices working to provide appropriate and meaningful educational programming for students with disabilities and their families.

Titles in Series:

The Essentials of Special Education Law
by David F. Bateman and Andrew M. Markelz

Special Education Law Annual Review 2020
by Mitchell L. Yell, David F. Bateman, and Kevin P. Brady

Developing Educationally Meaningful and Legally Sound IEPs
by David F. Bateman, Mitchell L. Yell, and James G. Shriner

Sexuality Education for Students with Disabilities
by Thomas Gibbon, Elizabeth Harkins Monaco, and David Bateman

Service Animals in Schools
by Anne O. Papalia, Kathy B. Ewoldt, and David F. Bateman

Creating Positive Elementary Classrooms
by Stephen W. Smith and Mitchell L. Yell

SERVICE ANIMALS IN SCHOOLS

LEGAL, EDUCATIONAL, ADMINISTRATIVE, AND STRATEGIC HANDLING ASPECTS

ANNE O. PAPALIA
Shippensburg University

KATHY B. EWOLDT
University of Texas–San Antonio

DAVID F. BATEMAN
Shippensburg University

ROWMAN & LITTLEFIELD
Lanham • Boulder • New York • London

Acquisitions Editor: Courtney Packard
Sales and Marketing Inquiries: textbooks@rowman.com

Credits and acknowledgments for material borrowed from other sources, and reproduced with permission, appear on the appropriate pages within the text.

Published by Rowman & Littlefield
An imprint of The Rowman & Littlefield Publishing Group, Inc.
4501 Forbes Boulevard, Suite 200, Lanham, Maryland 20706
www.rowman.com

86-90 Paul Street, London EC2A 4NE

Copyright © 2022 by The Rowman & Littlefield Publishing Group, Inc.

All rights reserved. No part of this book may be reproduced in any form or by any electronic or mechanical means, including information storage and retrieval systems, without written permission from the publisher, except by a reviewer who may quote passages in a review.

British Library Cataloguing in Publication Information Available

Library of Congress Cataloging-in-Publication Data
Names: Papalia, Anne O., 1962– author. | Ewoldt, Kathy B., 1969– author. | Bateman, David, 1963– author.
Title: Service animals in schools : a comprehensive guide for administrators, teachers, parents, and students / Anne O. Papalia, Kathy B. Ewoldt, David F. Bateman.
Description: Lanham, Maryland : Rowman & Littlefield, 2022. | Series: Special education law, policy, and practice | Includes bibliographical references and index.
Identifiers: LCCN 2022014050 (print) | LCCN 2022014051 (ebook) | ISBN 9781538158203 (cloth) | ISBN 9781538158210 (paperback) | ISBN 9781538158227 (epub)
Subjects: LCSH: Animals in education—United States. | Children with disabilities—Education—United States. | Animals as aids for people with disabilities—United States. | Emotional support animals—United States.
Classification: LCC LB1044.9.A65 P36 2022 (print) | LCC LB1044.9.A65 (ebook) | DDC 371.33—dc23/eng/20220511
LC record available at https://lccn.loc.gov/2022014050
LC ebook record available at https://lccn.loc.gov/2022014051

BRIEF CONTENTS

Chapter 1	Introduction	1
Chapter 2	History and Function of Service Animals in the United States	5
Chapter 3	Legal Definitions and Protection	11
Chapter 4	Types of Service Animals and Other Assistance Animals	27
Chapter 5	Service Animal Training and Acquisition	37
Chapter 6	Service Animals in Schools	53
Chapter 7	Service Animals, Students with Disabilities, and Special Education	69
Chapter 8	IEPs and Service Animals	75
Chapter 9	Service Animals in School: Implications for Administrators, Teachers, and Parents	91
Chapter 10	Addressing and Remediating Service Dog Issues	103
Chapter 11	Self-Advocacy Skills	117
Chapter 12	Transition Planning for Individuals with Service Animals	131
Chapter 13	Summary, Implications, and a Look Forward	143
Appendix 1	DOJ and Service Animals	153
Appendix 2	Sample School Policy	165
Bibliography		173
Index		179

CONTENTS

CHAPTER 1: INTRODUCTION — 1
Legal Aspects — 2
Educational and Accessibility Aspects — 3
Strategic Handling Aspects — 4
Summary — 4

CHAPTER 2: HISTORY AND FUNCTION OF SERVICE ANIMALS IN THE UNITED STATES — 5
Early Service Animals — 6
Becoming Service Dogs — 6
Legal Protection — 8
Human-Animal Bond — 8
Service Animal Expansion and Diversification — 9
Summary — 10

CHAPTER 3: LEGAL DEFINITIONS AND PROTECTION — 11
Definition of a Service Animal — 11
   28 CFR § 35.136—Service Animals — 11
Tasks a Service Animal Can Perform — 13
Service Animal vs. Emotional Support Animal — 14
Service Animal vs. Psychiatric Service Animal — 15
Training of Service Animals — 16
Service Dogs — 17
Service Dogs vs. Miniature Horses — 17
What Can a Service Horse Do? — 18
Other Animals? — 20
Title II and Schools — 20
Service Animal Removal — 20
Service Animal Handlers — 21
Serction 504 — 21
   What Is Section 504? — 21
   Section 504 and Service Animals — 22
IDEA and Service Animals — 23
   How Do I Know If a Service Animal Is Necessary for a FAPE? — 23
Employees with Service Animals — 24
Summary — 25

CHAPTER 4: TYPES OF SERVICE ANIMALS AND OTHER ASSISTANCE ANIMALS — 27
Assistance Animals — 28
   Service Animals — 29
   Therapy Animals — 30
   Emotional Support Animals — 32
Assistance Animal Legal Protections — 32
   Americans with Disabilities Act (ADA) — 33
   Fair Housing Act (FHA) — 34
   Air Carrier Access Act — 34
   Other Considerations — 35
Summary — 36

CHAPTER 5: SERVICE ANIMAL TRAINING AND ACQUISITION — 37
Questions to Ask — 38
   Question 1: Why? — 38
   Question 2: Why? Part 2 — 39
   Question 3: How? — 39
   Question 4: Space? — 40
   Question 5: Other Animals? — 40
   Question 6: Others for Advice? — 41
   Question 7: Finances? — 41
   Question 8: Finances? Part 2 — 42
   Question 9: Finances? Part 3 — 45
Lack of Regulation — 45
Questions to Ask of the Trainer — 46
Training for the Handler or Person with a Disability — 47
   Requalification Requirements — 48
   Introduction and Transition — 49
   Living with a Service Animal — 49
   Accreditation — 50
   Actual Places — 51
Summary — 51

CHAPTER 6: SERVICE ANIMALS IN SCHOOLS — 53
Framework for Determining Service Animal Access — 56
   Step 1: Determining Service Dog Status — 56
   Step 2: Determining the Role of the Handler — 58
   Step 3: Determining Legal Protection Afforded — 59

Strategic Handling Skills 61
Prior Notice 61
Legal and Service Dog Etiquette Information 62
Environmental Assessments 63
Summary 63

CHAPTER 7: SERVICE ANIMALS, STUDENTS WITH DISABILITIES, AND SPECIAL EDUCATION **69**
Dual Protection: IDEA vs. ADA and 504 69
Purpose 69
Eligibility 70
Educational Responsibilities 70
Evaluation 71
Placement 71
Service Animals and Dually Protected Students 72
Summary 73

CHAPTER 8: IEPs AND SERVICE ANIMALS **75**
Law Review 75
Components of the IEP 77
Writing Legally Defensible IEPs 78
The Process 78
Progress 81
Suggested IEP Practices 82
IEP Development Is a Student-Driven Process 82
Placement 83
Teams Must Do the Right Thing 84
Key Elements of the IEP Process 84
Service Animals 84
IEPs and Service Animals 86
Tips for School Districts under IDEA for Service Animals 86
Summary 89

CHAPTER 9: SERVICE ANIMALS IN SCHOOL: IMPLICATIONS FOR ADMINISTRATORS, TEACHERS, AND PARENTS **91**
Policies 91
Planning for a Service Animal 92
Animal 92
People 94

Training	95
Mitigation	96
What Parents Should Know	97
Notification	97
Advocacy	98
Logistics	98
Appendix: Sample Service Dog Letter to Parents	102

CHAPTER 10: ADDRESSING AND REMEDIATING SERVICE DOG ISSUES — 103

Proactive Problem Solving	104
Understanding Service Animal Expectations	104
Service Dog Criteria	105
Health Issues	106
Implications of Service Dog Expectations	106
Addressing Minor Problems	107
Major Issues: Loss of Control and Removal	109
Determining Out-of-Control Behavior	109
Addressing Out-of-Control Behavior	110
Summary	113

CHAPTER 11: SELF-ADVOCACY SKILLS — 117

Problems Encountered by Service Dog Users	118
Legal-Based Issues	119
Preconceived View of Service Animals	119
Interaction-Based Issues	122
Self-Advocacy Techniques	123
Legal Self-Advocacy	123
Interaction Self-Advocacy	126
Advocating for the Whole Team	127
Summary	128

CHAPTER 12: TRANSITION PLANNING FOR INDIVIDUALS WITH SERVICE ANIMALS — 131

What Is Transition?	132
IDEA Transition Components	133
Transition to Employment	134
Environmental Analysis	134
Legal Knowledge and Self-Advocacy	136

Transition to Postsecondary Education 137
   Bringing a Service Dog to College 138
   College-Specific Aspects of Transition 139
Summary 141

CHAPTER 13: SUMMARY, IMPLICATIONS, AND A LOOK FORWARD 143
Lessons Learned from This Case: Summary and Implications 144
   Legal, Educational, and Access Issues 144
   Important Legal, Access, and Educational Considerations 145
   Addressing Problems 148
   Strategic Handling 150
Summary 152

Appendix 1: DOJ and Service Animals 153
Appendix 2: Sample School Policy 165
Bibliography 173
Index 179

CHAPTER 1

INTRODUCTION

> School personnel are often confronted with the task of determining the extent of access a service dog and handler have to school buildings in general and the classrooms in particular. The determination is based on multiple factors. Legal, educational, and access issues must be considered.
> —Anne O. Papalia, "Service Dogs in Schools"

ADVANCED ORGANIZER

After reading this chapter, you will be able to:

- describe the current status of service animal use,
- understand the legal definition of service animals,
- identify the function of service animals based on the legal definition,
- understand policies and practices involved in using service animals in schools, and
- recognize the need for strategic handling of service animals in the school environment.

IS THAT DOG ALLOWED IN SCHOOL? Can the miniature horse ride on the bus with my son? Must the service animal leave the classroom if the teacher is allergic? Do I need to include the service animal in the IEP? These are some of the many questions that exist when a child with a disability brings a service animal to school. *Service Animals in Schools: Legal, Educational, Administrative, and Strategic Handling Aspects* raises and answers these questions and several more as we consider the multitude of considerations and perspectives around service animals in schools.

The purpose of this book is to provide a comprehensive guide for service animal use in schools. We address the legal components regarding the definition of service animals and the access provided to them within schools. We also discuss the educational components involving the specific use of service animals in schools and special education planning and delivery. We present strategic handling issues regarding situations handlers encounter while using their service animals. This book is unique in that it explores topics involved at both ends of the leash.

The information provided in this book is important for several reasons. The use of service animals in society overall and within schools in particular is increasing within the United States. The types of support provided by service animals and the names used to identify them have expanded as well. At the same time, the use of other types of assistance animals, such as therapy animals and emotional support animals, has increased. The rise of service and assistance animals in public has prompted many recent court cases, changes to state laws, and updates to federal regulations. Increased usage has also prompted confusion regarding the legal status and access rights afforded to each type of animal. Because there is an increased demand for animals in public places, it is safe to say there is an increased need for people who visit educational settings to become familiar with animals in public. These individuals include students, parents, visitors, teachers, employees, administrators, paraprofessionals, related-service providers, and a number of other stakeholders who visit, work, or play at educational sites. This chapter will introduce you to some of the key content we hope to convey is this book.

LEGAL ASPECTS

Presently, the laws that govern animal rights, protections, and allowances vary by country. Within the United States, though we have federal laws, there are differences by state, and there is much confusion around terminology of animals encountered in our daily lives. When you consider the term *service animal*, what picture does your mind conjure? The answer will vary greatly depending on your background experiences. These experiences also drive our understanding of the various terms used to describe animals that provide benefit to people such as *service, assistance, therapy, emotional support,* and others. For our purposes, we imply the legal definition when we use the term *service animal*. A service animal is a dog (or a miniature horse) that is specifically trained to perform a disability-related task for its handler (Americans with Disabilities Act [ADA], 1990). An in-depth discussion of service animal definitions is included within chapter 3 of this text. Chapter 4 includes information on the other types of assistance animals and how they differ from service animals.

There are surprisingly few regulations regarding registration and certification of service animals in the United States. Specific training is required for an animal to be considered a service animal. This training need not be formal; individuals can self-train their dog or miniature horse to perform a disability-related task. If an individual chooses formal training, they may seek an animal that is already trained to be a service animal, or they may acquire their animal first and then have it professionally trained. Regardless of whether the animal is owner trained or acquired from a facility, there are several factors to consider for individuals and families contemplating a service animal. Information regarding considerations, acquisition, and training of service animals is provided in chapter 5.

EDUCATIONAL AND ACCESSIBILITY ASPECTS

Service animals affect educational environments whenever a student, employee, or other community member with a service animal enters a school setting, which leads to questions of access. Are there legal requirements for access? If not, are there moral or ethical obligations to allow access? The lack of service animal oversight combined with the misunderstanding of assistance animal terminology confound these questions. As leaders grapple with these decisions and other stakeholders weigh in on the conversations, chapter 6 provides a three-step framework to guide this process.

When it comes to looking specifically at children with disabilities in school settings, there are three major laws that affect educational settings: Section 504 of the Rehabilitation Act of 1973, the Americans with Disabilities Act (ADA), and the Individuals with Disabilities Education Act (IDEA). Each of these laws may be part of the conversation around service animals in school and, depending on the specific situation, have impact to varying degrees. The impact of a disability is quite individualized, and no instances will be exactly aligned. In this same way, the unique situation that necessitates a service animal will be individualized. Thus the appropriate and applicable laws may each apply or may apply in tandem with the others. We provide an extensive discussion of Section 504, ADA, IDEA, and the implications these mandates have on students with disabilities who have service animals. When a student qualifies for special education services, we further discuss the impact service animals have on developing and implementing a student's Individualized Education Program.

Educational and accessibility aspects of service animals on campus are topics that will be important and relevant to a variety of stakeholders. Administrators who lead schools, regions, or districts are provided with implications of service animals on Individualized Education Programs in chapter 8 and thought-provoking content to consider as they lead their respective sites.

Leadership personnel will find policy development and communication tools in chapter 9 and problem-resolution suggestions in chapter 10. Parents are also provided specific considerations in chapter 9. Related service providers, teachers, counselors, and other school staff will also find the information in this section beneficial in understanding their roles and expectations regarding service animals in educational settings.

STRATEGIC HANDLING ASPECTS

Students who have service animals will encounter a variety of situations while attending school. These may be logistical in nature, or possibly they will face resistance to the presence of their animal. We discuss ways to address and remediate issues with service animals in the classroom in chapter 10 and present self-advocating and advocacy of service animals in general in chapter 11. We also provide discussions for transition planning when students move to a different school or move on to secondary education. For students who have a service animal, their educational considerations move forward and continue beyond their graduation. Whether the student chooses to enter the workforce or attend postsecondary schools such as career technical centers, community college, college, or university, their service animal provides a level of independence that would otherwise not be possible. They have become a team, and as the team graduates, there are planning considerations that will help to ease the transition into their next great endeavor. Chapter 12 helps to guide these plans. In the final chapter, we consider a variety of implications related to service animals that all stakeholders will continue to grapple with, including the importance of protecting the rights of individuals and animals who are legitimately teamed in service.

SUMMARY

In the chapters ahead, we provide a comprehensive blend of legal, administrative, and educational information with practical guidelines for addressing these issues within the school setting. We explore service animals' issues from the administrator, teacher, parent, and service animal handler point of view. We address topics such as legal access, types of assistance animals, educational planning and IEP development, classroom integration, transition planning with a service animal, and service dog advocacy skills. Overall, the purpose of this book is to explore service animal use in schools from both ends of the leash.

CHAPTER 2

HISTORY AND FUNCTION OF SERVICE ANIMALS IN THE UNITED STATES

Every creature was designed to serve a purpose. Learn from animals for they are there to teach you the way of life. There is a wealth of knowledge that is openly accessible in nature. Our ancestors knew this and embraced the natural cures found in the bosoms of the earth. Their classroom was nature. They studied the lessons to be learned from animals. Much of human behavior can be explained by watching the wild beasts around us. They are constantly teaching us things about ourselves and the way of the universe, but most people are too blind to watch and listen.
—Suzy Kassem, *Rise Up and Salute the Sun: The Writings of Suzy Kassem*

> **ADVANCED ORGANIZER**
>
> Upon completing this chapter, you will be able to describe:
>
> - the evolution of service animals use in the United States,
> - examples of early service animals,
> - the acceptance of animals as service animals,
> - the current growth and diversification of service,
> - the expansion of the therapy dog movement,
> - the importance of the human-animal bond and its emergence as a research area, and
> - the expansion and diversity of service dog use.

ANIMALS HAVE BEEN an integral part of human history for thousands of years (Kalof, 2007). Species such as dogs have been used by humans throughout history for companionship, hunting, herding, sport and recreation, security, protection, and emotional support. Historically, as animal usage in varying fields of science has increased, so has the availability of animal history risen (Riveto, 2002). The use of animals to assist people with physical and psychiatric disabilities also is noted across time but has rapidly increased recently in the United States (Parenti et al., 2013). The purpose of the chapter is to describe the evolution of service animals used to support people with disabilities and provide information regarding how service dogs have become more prevalent in the lives of individuals with disabilities. This chapter is not designed to argue for or against animal agency nor discuss ideological notions related to the subjectivity of nonhuman animals to the benefit of humans.

EARLY SERVICE ANIMALS

Animals are portrayed in many ancient works of art with the appearance of service animals in works dating back to the early 1600s in Rembrandt's *The Blind Fiddler* and Callot's *L'aveugle et son chien* (The Blind Man and His Dog; Malamud, 2013). In colonial America, dogs can be seen as companions in art. However, in some circles animals were portrayed negatively, seen as demonic vessels, and used as evidence of witchcraft, which was a sin punishable by death (Brooks, 2012).

Animals have helped improve the lives of humans for generations by making agricultural work easier, providing transportation (e.g., chariots, stagecoaches), and providing comfort to soldiers on the front line. During World War I, dogs were trained to perform search and recovery operations (Greatbatch et al., 2015) and to rid trenches of rat infestation (Monovisions, 2018); in World War II dogs sniffed out landmines (Kirk, 2014). Dogs have been used for tasks such as herding, hunting, and transport (Reisen, 2018). Training dogs to perform specific tasks for people with disabilities originated in Europe as early as the late 1700s.

The relationship between service animal and handler is not solely one-sided, with the power and benefit skewed towards the handler. The success of guide dogs as service animals is dependent upon the notion that dogs have a desire to please their human companion. It stems from an emotional need for attention, which is required for successful relationships (Odendaal, 2000). The dog's desire to please their handler and the handler's need for assistance creates an interdependence. When the needs of each are well matched, there is a successful companionship. A dog breed that desires to please humans is a basic need for the coconstructed, interdependent relationship between animal and handler. If the dog has no motivation for human acceptance and approval, there will be difficulty in training and the dog's ability to provide service over the long term.

BECOMING SERVICE DOGS

Dogs serving individuals with disabilities in the United States began in the late 1920s (The Seeing Eye, n.d.). Two Americans were drawn to the dog training occurring in Europe at the time. Dorothy Eustis, an animal researcher in New York, was intrigued by the training dogs received to serve the Swiss military. While in Europe, she traveled to Germany after learning of dogs that were being trained to serve blinded war veterans. So moved by the change in confidence, countenance, mobility, and independence men regained after pairing with their "shepherd dog," Ms. Eustis returned to Switzerland and started her own training program. She published an article in the *Saturday Evening Post* in 1927 (Nilsson, Hollandbeck, and Eustis, 2016), prompting Mr. Morris Frank, a nineteen-year-old who had acquired blindness three years prior and was desperate to regain his independence, to write to Ms. Eustis (https://www.seeingeye.org/assets/pdfs/history/morris-franks-letter.pdf). In his request letter to Eustis, Frank stated he wanted to spread this work in America to replace what he felt was an ill-desired dependence on another human being for guidance. Having a firsthand experience of losing independence due to blindness, he desired to share the regained livelihood having a service dog could provide to so many others who were also blind.

In the mid-1970s, Dr. Bonnie Bergin was traveling abroad and noticed donkeys assisting people with disabilities. Like Ms. Eustis, Dr. Bergin's visionary approach led to training dogs to provide mobility services to individuals with disabilities. Dr. Bergin was first to coin the term *service dog* in an effort to distinguish dogs that were specifically trained to provide service compared to other assistance animals or pets (Franke, 2020). Her testimony before Congress was instrumental in the development of the Americans with Disabilities Act of 1990. Although animals have "served" humans for many years, the United States did not officially recognize service animals by providing legal protections until 1990 with the passage of the Americans with Disabilities Act.

As an alternative to service dogs, the training of miniature horses began in the late 1990s when Janet Burleson, a show-horse trainer from North Carolina with three decades of experience, was inspired by a horse ride in New York City (Peterson, 2003). An observer of horse behavior, Burleson noticed how remarkably well the horses navigated the city bustle, including an almost instinctive understanding of when it was safe to cross busy streets. Her experiences led her to wonder if miniature horses could be trained to serve as guides for people who are blind. Upon return from the business trip, she began training her own miniature horse. In 2001, a man in his forties, with acquired blindness at the age of seventeen, volunteered to be the first handler to be paired with a miniature horse trained by Burleson. Dan Shaw had spent years battling the emotional toll of feeling isolated and inadequate. Having experienced the loss of a dog in childhood, he did not want to suffer that loss again and avoided pairing with a seeing-eye dog.

Shaw knew the bond between handler and service animal could be much stronger compared to the bond with his pet dog, and he was not willing to accept that experience again, let alone the four-plus times it might occur over his lifetime. However, when he heard about the longevity of a miniature horse, he reached out to Burleson. After the initial success with Shaw and "Cuddles," Burleson started the Guide Horse Foundation, which continues to train mini's today.

LEGAL PROTECTION

Animal protection legislation is not a new concept. Litigation in the United States involving animals can be traced back to the early years of the nation. For example, in the 1805 case of *Pierson v. Post*, two men were hunting the same fox. Post was the first to make a chase and used that fact to claim ownership despite Pierson's shot that killed the fox. The courts sided with Pierson ruling that animal possession begins at full capture or killing. In the nineteenth century, the notion that animals feel pain and emotion gave rise to society's consideration of how animals should be treated, which led to litigation reflecting cultural beliefs (Kelch, 2013). For example, the Human Methods of Livestock Slaughter Act of 1958 and the Marine Mammal Protection Act of 1972 have protected animals from human mistreatment and depletion. Additional animal rights legislation emerged from the 1970s to late 1980s (see Tischler, 2008) but it was not until the passage of the Americans with Disabilities Act of 1990 that service animals and their handlers were afforded legal protections (see chapter 3).

HUMAN-ANIMAL BOND

Prior to the development of legal protections for service animals, research was occurring supporting the human-animal bond. The human-animal bond has existed for centuries (Serpell, 2015). This special relationship between people and their animals is based on mutually beneficial companionship. Research in this area elevated the role of animals as helpers within society.

Research on how to best incorporate animals in therapeutic ways for the psychological and physical benefits they provide began in the mid-twentieth century and was pioneered by Boris Levinson. Acting on his own experiences with his dog, Jingles, and the responses of the children in the therapy clinic, he proposed using dogs as "co-therapists" (Levinson, 1962, p. 64). He recognized how otherwise withdrawn children became relaxed and engaged in the presence of Jingles and saw these interactions as a springboard to develop a trusting relationship between client and therapist.

Psychiatrists Samuel and Elizabeth Corson expanded on Levinson's work by empirically investigating the impact of their "pet-facilitated psychotherapy" in the psychiatric unit at the Ohio State University (Corson et al., 1977, p. 62). Noncommunicative patients cared for dogs used within a nearby laboratory. Results supported Levinson's findings that the dogs became "social catalysts, forging positive links between the subject and other patients and staff on the ward, and thus creating a widening circle of warmth and acceptance" (Serpell, 2015, pp. 8–9).

These works promulgated the idea of animal-assisted interventions, although not specifically named as such, as being extremely beneficial and effective. Researchers across a wide variety of domains and nations examined these benefits in the late 1970s and 1980s (Serpell, 2015). Out of these works came the basis of animal-assisted therapy (AAT) and animal-assisted activities (AAA). AAT is intervention-based. It involves using a therapy animal within a specific intervention in a goal-directed way under the guidance of a therapist. AAA is recreational in nature. Therapy animals are used within motivational, educational, or recreational activities to enhance quality of life. Additional information regarding the definition and implementation of AAT and AAA is included in chapter 4.

As interest in AAT and AAA spread, organizations to support their implementation emerged. Therapy Dogs International (TDI) was founded in 1976 by Elaine Smith in New Jersey (Therapy Dogs International, n.d.). By organizing, TDI united people who wanted to expand the beneficial use of volunteer therapy dogs. TDI developed evaluation criteria used to certify therapy dogs and their handlers. Delta Society was established in 1977 in Eugene, Oregon (Pet Partners, 2021). Dedicated to researching and promoting the value of the human-animal bond, this organization has become a clearinghouse for information on the benefits of service animals and therapy animals. It developed the Pet Partners program. Additional therapy dog organizations have emerged, including Therapy Dog Alliance (formally known as Therapy Dog Incorporated).

SERVICE ANIMAL EXPANSION AND DIVERSIFICATION

The recognition of animal-assisted therapy as an intervention has resulted in the presence of animals in a variety of settings, including schools. The expanded use of therapy animals has helped inform and legitimize the use of service animals to perform a variety of functions for people with disabilities. As previously mentioned, in the past, service animals assisted people with visual impairments as guide dogs or physical disabilities as mobility animals. These types of service animals not only aid their handlers' disability and provide greater independence, but they also promote self-confidence, peace of mind, a greater sense of safety, and enhanced social interaction, all elements associated with the human-animal bond. This broader range of benefits opened the door to other creative uses of dogs for people with disabilities such as their calming effect on individuals with trauma or sensory disabilities, alerting diabetics of a hypoglycemic episode, or alerting an individual of a forthcoming seizure (Walther et al., 2017).

The gradual acceptance of various forms of disability in society has also impacted the function and use of service animals. Walther and colleagues (2017) conducted a historical analysis of service dog preparation facilities based on function across time. Findings indicate that prior to the 1980s, facilities primarily trained dogs for individuals with overt physical disabilities such as visual impairments or mobility disabilities. In the 1990s, an increasing number of facilities began training dogs to assist children with autism. In the early 2000s, the number of facilities training diabetic and seizure alert dogs and psychiatric service dogs increased. These findings project an overall trend moving from using service dogs to support visible disabilities such as sensory and physical impairment, to invisible disabilities including psychiatric and medical disabilities. The timeline also suggests an expanding age range across handlers with the introduction of service animals trained to support children with autism. These trends have implications for increasing numbers of service animals in schools.

SUMMARY

The positive impact of animals on their human counterparts has been recognized across multiple centuries. The support animals provide has slowly shifted from meeting essential human needs and direct support to people with disabilities. Researchers have explored the impact of the human-animal bond, and society has recognized the benefits of interacting with animals. The use of service animals by people with various disabilities has expanded as well. Society has provided legal protections for service animals and their handlers. More recently, the functions performed by service animals have increased. The types of disabilities mitigated through the use of service animals also have expanded. These historical trends have implications for the present and future. Service animals are increasingly present in everyday institutions of society, including schools.

CHAPTER 3

LEGAL DEFINITIONS AND PROTECTION

This chapter will cover the specific federal regulations related to service animals as they are addressed in the Americans with Disabilities Act (ADA), the Individuals with Disabilities Education Act (IDEA), and Section 504 of the Rehabilitation Act. It will also seek to address how they are intertwined and the specific responsibilities that schools have related to the provision of service animals. To reduce any miscommunication, there will be multiple direct citations to the federal regulations when necessary. We have also provided as an appendix to this book a good reference from the US Department of Justice on frequently asked questions on service animals. We highly recommend you read that as well. As we address the specifics of the regulations, we will also periodically provide commentary to assist the reader with understanding the implications and expectations of schools as related to service animals. The regulations are a main component of how schools should operate related to service animals, but what does this really mean for day-to-day school operations?

DEFINITION OF A SERVICE ANIMAL

To ensure there is no dispute about what we are addressing, we would like to highlight the specific federal regulations relating to the definition of a service animal. We will then work to explain those regulations and provide guidance for schools.

28 CFR § 35.136—Service Animals

(a) General. Generally, a public entity shall modify its policies, practices, or procedures to permit the use of a service animal by an individual with a disability.
(b) Exceptions. A public entity may ask an individual with a disability to remove a service animal from the premises if -
  (1) The animal is out of control and the animal's handler does not take effective action to control it; or
  (2) The animal is not housebroken.

(c) If an animal is properly excluded. If a public entity properly excludes a service animal under § 35.136(b), it shall give the individual with a disability the opportunity to participate in the service, program, or activity without having the service animal on the premises.

(d) Animal under handler's control. A service animal shall be under the control of its handler. A service animal shall have a harness, leash, or other tether, unless either the handler is unable because of a disability to use a harness, leash, or other tether, or the use of a harness, leash, or other tether would interfere with the service animal's safe, effective performance of work or tasks, in which case the service animal must be otherwise under the handler's control (e.g., voice control, signals, or other effective means).

(e) Care or supervision. A public entity is not responsible for the care or supervision of a service animal.

(f) Inquiries. A public entity shall not ask about the nature or extent of a person's disability, but may make two inquiries to determine whether an animal qualifies as a service animal. A public entity may ask if the animal is required because of a disability and what work or task the animal has been trained to perform. A public entity shall not require documentation, such as proof that the animal has been certified, trained, or licensed as a service animal. Generally, a public entity may not make these inquiries about a service animal when it is readily apparent that an animal is trained to do work or perform tasks for an individual with a disability (e.g., the dog is observed guiding an individual who is blind or has low vision, pulling a person's wheelchair, or providing assistance with stability or balance to an individual with an observable mobility disability).

(g) Access to areas of a public entity. Individuals with disabilities shall be permitted to be accompanied by their service animals in all areas of a public entity's facilities where members of the public, participants in services, programs or activities, or invitees, as relevant, are allowed to go.

(h) Surcharges. A public entity shall not ask or require an individual with a disability to pay a surcharge, even if people accompanied by pets are required to pay fees, or to comply with other requirements generally not applicable to people without pets. If a public entity normally charges individuals for the damage they cause, an individual with a disability may be charged for damage caused by his or her service animal.

(i) Miniature horses.
    (1) Reasonable modifications. A public entity shall make reasonable modifications in policies, practices, or procedures to permit the use of a miniature horse by an individual with a disability if the miniature

horse has been individually trained to do work or perform tasks for the benefit of the individual with a disability.
(2) Assessment factors. In determining whether reasonable modifications in policies, practices, or procedures can be made to allow a miniature horse into a specific facility, a public entity shall consider -
   (i) The type, size, and weight of the miniature horse and whether the facility can accommodate these features;
   (ii) Whether the handler has sufficient control of the miniature horse;
   (iii) Whether the miniature horse is housebroken; and
   (iv) Whether the miniature horse's presence in a specific facility compromises legitimate safety requirements that are necessary for safe operation.
(3) Other requirements. Paragraphs 35.136(c) through (h) of this section, which apply to service animals, shall also apply to miniature horses.

[AG Order No. 3180-2010, 75 FR 56178, Sept. 15, 2010; 76 FR 13285, Mar. 11, 2011]

TASKS A SERVICE ANIMAL CAN PERFORM

There are not specific regulations about the tasks that a service animal can perform. There may be state guidance on such, but we would like to highlight some of the specifics now that we have identified what precisely is a service animal. We will get into further definitions below on the different types. The tasks that a service animal can perform depend on the unique needs of the individual and of the training of the animal. The following is a list of tasks published by the ADA National Network, which provides information, guidance, and training on the ADA (https://ADATA.org).

The work or tasks performed by a service animal must be directly related to the individual's disability. Examples of work or tasks include but are not limited to:

- assisting individuals who are blind or have low vision with navigation and other tasks,
- alerting individuals who are deaf or hard of hearing to the presence of people or sounds,
- providing nonviolent protection or rescue work,
- pulling a wheelchair,
- assisting an individual during a seizure,

- alerting individuals to the presence of allergens,
- retrieving items such as medicine or the telephone,
- providing physical support and assistance with balance and stability to individuals with mobility disabilities, and
- helping individuals with psychiatric and neurological disabilities by preventing or interrupting impulsive or destructive behaviors.

The crime deterrent effects of an animal's presence and the provision of emotional support, well-being, comfort, or companionship are not considered work or tasks under the definition of a service animal.

This list of tasks is broad in nature, affecting the public at large. For schools, the list of tasks is not different, but schools need to work with the student to assist when there is a need expressed. If a student expresses a need for a service animal, this is a notice to the school that this student may require additional supports. When this occurs, the school district has an affirmative obligation to determine if this student's needs rise to the level of requiring special education services.

SERVICE ANIMAL VS. EMOTIONAL SUPPORT ANIMAL

Before we clarify the difference, allow us to define emotional support animal. For most people who have a pet, the animal provides comfort and companionship. Typically, these pets have an emotional connection with their owner. For many people, this is a huge benefit to having a pet, and this alone provides great comfort. There are differences, however, between a pet and an emotional support animal (ESA). To be considered an emotional support animal, the pet needs to be prescribed by a licensed mental health professional to a person with a disabling mental illness. A licensed therapist, psychologist, or psychiatrist must determine the presence of the animal is needed for the continuing and ongoing mental health of the individual. There are many examples of this. Having an ESA dog might assist with issues related to depression; an ESA might assist with issues related to anxiety in crowded places; the ESA could assist the individual with certain phobias or fears; or the ESA could just provide the companionship necessary for an individual after the death of a loved one. There are many different roles ESAs may play in a person's life. Finally, there are no specific guidelines or requirements about the breed, size, or age of the animal. For more specific guidelines about the differences between service animals and emotional support animals, the reader is referred to the *Federal Register*, volume 75, number 178, pages 56193–95 (September 15, 2010).

Given the definition of an ESA, what is the difference between that and a service animal? First, emotional support animals do not receive the same legal protections as service animals, and as a result, owners of ESAs do not receive the same accommodations for their animals as owners of service animals. A service dog, such as a guide dog, is typically allowed anywhere the public is allowed, as opposed to emotional service animals, which are not allowed. This is not just in schools, as ESAs generally cannot accompany their owners into grocery stores, shopping malls, or restaurants. Why the difference? The ADA defines service animals as "dogs individually trained to do work or perform tasks for people with disabilities." Dogs that only provide emotional support services are not included as a part of this definition. As we note on all discussions related to laws, localities may have different rules and requirements; the defining point comes down to whether the animal has been trained to perform a specific task or job directly related to the person's disability. Service dogs are trained for very specific tasks to assist a person with a disability; dogs that are trained to only provide comfort, though often much appreciated, are not part of this definition.

SERVICE ANIMAL VS. PSYCHIATRIC SERVICE ANIMAL

Different from emotional service animals, psychiatric service animals are trained for specific tasks and therefore can be labeled as a service animal, and the owner receives all the rights and responsibilities that go along with a service animal. To be eligible for a psychiatric service dog, a person must be diagnosed by a licensed professional with a mental health condition that requires assistance. Service dogs for people with psychiatric disabilities are specially trained to perform tasks that mitigate a person's disability. While important, just providing comfort, such as by an emotional service animal (see above), does not qualify the dog as a service dog. Again, for more specific guidelines about the differences between service animals and psychiatric support animals, the reader is referred to the *Federal Register*, volume 75, number 178, pages 56193–95 (September 15, 2010).

There are many different tasks that psychiatric service animals can do to assist a person with their needs. The tasks include:

- getting help,
- waking a person from nightmares,
- waking a person when the alarm sounds,
- balance assistance,

- being a medication reminder,
- retrieving medication,
- retrieving water bottles,
- providing tactical stimulation,
- serving as a buffer in crowded situations,
- calming a person down when agitated,
- creating a personal space that is safe,
- disrupting emotional overload, and
- stopping self-mutilation or other destructive behaviors.

TRAINING OF SERVICE ANIMALS

Some dogs have over the years been bred to be better at some innate tasks. For example, retriever breeds including Labradors instinctively fetch, guardian breeds like rottweilers instinctively protect, and border collies instinctively herd. This innate instinct is good for the specific skill but is not necessarily good for a service dog. Even though these dogs may be smart and good at what they do, service dog training can take up to two intensive years. While in training, these dogs usually wear a vest in public to allow for easy identification. There are no specifics for which breeds can become a service animal. Any dog can enter service dog training, regardless of breed or age. It is important to realize that, unless they have a certain set of characteristics, they might not do well.

Service dog characteristics include:

- willing to please,
- calm,
- friendly,
- alert,
- socialized,
- quick learner,
- ready to follow owners everywhere, and
- nonreactive to public and strangers.

Types of service animals include:

Hearing Dogs
- Warn about vehicles
- Alert to sounds
- Alert to alarms
- Alert to other people

Guide Dogs
- Assist with getting around obstacles
- Assist with steps/inclines/declines/holes
- Retrieval of objects

SERVICE DOGS

There are many tasks service dogs can perform in addition to the ones above. The important skills are the ones necessary to assist with independence for the individual with a disability. The service animal may be a guide dog, a hearing dog, or a psychiatric service animal. All are specifically trained to provide guidance and assistance for the person, with each being specifically trained and targeted for the person's individual needs.

There is no specific national certifying organization for the training of a service animal, and there are no specific regulations regarding service dog training. Appropriate training requires time and dedicated practice. A low standard is 120 hours of training for the dog (*Federal Register*, volume 75, number 178 [September 15, 2010]). This training would also occur over a period of more than six months and not just over a few weeks, as the practice and repetition of skills over time is necessary to assist the dog in mastering the tasks for which they will be responsible. Additionally, future service animals should receive more than thirty hours of direct training in working in the public and accessing and moving around in public spaces. Finally, the specifics of the training are dependent on the breed, the individual dog, and the specialized skills we are expecting them to master.

SERVICE DOGS VS. MINIATURE HORSES

When one thinks of service animals, typically the only animal one considers is a dog. Service dogs are by far the majority of service animals. In fact, most people when considering the possibility of service do not consider other animals and especially would not consider a miniature horse as a service animal. However, there is a small percentage of service animals that are miniature horses. Although not included in the definition of a service animal, miniature horses are specifically listed in the regulations as the one animal that may be used as an exception to a dog. A miniature horse, then, meets the definition of a service animal when it has been individually trained to perform work or a specific task for the benefit of an individual with a disability.

Specifically:

> In addition to the provisions about service dogs, the Department's ADA regulations have a separate provision about miniature horses that have been individually trained to do work or perform tasks for people with disabilities. (Miniature horses generally range in height from 24 inches to 34 inches measured to the shoulders and generally weigh between 70 and 100 pounds.) Entities covered by the ADA must modify their policies to permit miniature horses where reasonable. (US Department of Justice, 2010)

Under the Americans with Disabilities Act, the new regulations state that places and policies that are already in place must now permit miniature horses, where reasonable, to be treated the same as dogs. The miniature horses should be twenty-four inches to thirty-four inches in height and weigh around seventy to one hundred pounds. As miniature horses are often much bigger than dogs, they have to follow more regulations to ensure they are providing a safe service to their owner as well as the people around them.

The regulations set out four assessment factors to assist entities in determining whether miniature horses can be accommodated in their facility. The assessment factors are:

- whether the miniature horse is housebroken;
- whether the miniature horse is under the owner's control;
- whether the facility can accommodate the miniature horse's type, size, and weight; and
- whether the miniature horse's presence will compromise legitimate safety requirements necessary for safe operation of the facility.

WHAT CAN A SERVICE HORSE DO?

Service horses are trained and can do the same work as a service dog. If there is one area where service horses are best suited, it is working as a guide to someone who is blind or has visual impairments. Some miniature horses also work very effectively as an emotional support animal (see emotional support animals above for more guidance on the applicable rules). Miniature horses are a lot less common as service animals and have not historically been used in this manner. The regulations recently changed, allowing miniature horses to be used as service animals, and with the correct training, they can work as effective guides.

Obviously not all horses meet the requirements for being a service animal. We are explicitly talking about miniature horses, not just small or young horses. All service horses must not only be trained to a high level but also possess good behavior and a clear ability to be under excellent control before they are considered. Just like service dogs, they need to be able to meet the needs of their individual owner.

There are several issues that need to be addressed specifically related to the use and training of miniature horses as service animals. First, as noted above, the training of the horse to be a service animal is intensive and needs to address the specific needs of the individual with a disability for whom they will be working. Different from dogs, however, is that miniature horse training may take longer because they tend to be more easily spooked by loud noises or crowds, much more so than dogs. Extreme reactions to this form of stimuli can be reduced through training, but it has to be considered as a major part of their training in addition to the other responsibilities they will have for the person with a disability. They also may require additional training in specific situations with the person with a disability, and this would include the house, shopping, likely places of travel, and work situations.

Second, an often not realized fact about service horses as compared to service dogs: despite the requirements for additional training necessary for social situations as mentioned above, the cost-benefit ratio of a service horse may be much more beneficial than one might think. As noted throughout this book, the service animal requires extensive training to be effective for the person with a disability. This is a major time commitment for all animals. But as a percentage of the animal's life, the service horse might be significantly cheaper in the long run as the service horse has a very different life expectancy.

Horses live a long time (up to thirty-five years) and can work for twenty or so years while providing support to their owners. Miniature horses are also a great size to support someone with a disability that impairs their mobility. Because they are at hip height and have a strong, well-built body, service horses are ideal for someone who is struggling with their mobility and often loses their balance. Additionally, miniature horses do not shed in the same manner as dogs and as such do not cause the same allergies that a dog might. Therefore, a service horse may be more appropriate for someone who has sensitivities to dog hair or fleas. Despite the sensitivities to loud noises as noted above, miniature horses can stand and wait for long periods of time, as opposed to some dogs, which may require more social interaction. Finally, there are some religions and cultures that do not value or allow dogs to be in houses, and that impediment does not exist for miniature horses.

OTHER ANIMALS?

Over the past few years, there has been a dramatic increase of fraudulent animals being used as service animals. For example, many airlines have recently asked the US Department of Justice to clarify that service animals are only dogs and not other animals (traveller.com, 2020). The Department of Justice in 2010 limited the definition of a service animal to dogs and miniature horses. However, other animals may be trained or could be successful in assisting individuals with disabilities. There is some evidence that small monkeys, especially the capuchin, could be trained to be a support animal as well, and there are websites where trained monkeys can be acquired for assistance (i.e., https://monkeyhelpers.org).

TITLE II AND SCHOOLS

Students with disabilities have the right to bring service animals to school. We will cover specifically the guidance provided by the Department of Justice related to Title II. Schools are Title II entities and therefore, "Title II entities have the same legal obligations as Title III entities to make reasonable modifications in policies, practices, or procedures to allow service animals when necessary in order to avoid discrimination on the basis of disability, unless the entity can demonstrate that making the modifications would fundamentally alter the nature of the service, program, or activity" (*Federal Register*, volume 75, number 178 [September 15, 2010], p. 56191).

What does this mean? Schools must modify their policies, practices, and procedures to permit the use of service animals by individuals with disabilities (28 CFR 35.136 (a)). Districts may not prohibit the use of service animals on school grounds. Schools also need to make sure that parents and members of the community believe service animals are welcome at schools.

SERVICE ANIMAL REMOVAL

We hope this is not necessary, but schools (and any other public entity) may ask for the removal of a service animal from the premises if:

1. the animal is out of control and the handler does not take effective action to control it; or
2. the animal is not housebroken (28 CFR 35.136 (b)).

If the service animal needs to be removed from the premises, the public entity *must* give the individual with a disability the opportunity to participate in the service, program, or activity without the service animal if the public entity properly excludes the animal from the premises (28 CFR 35.136 (c)).

SERVICE ANIMAL HANDLERS

A frequently forgotten aspect of the issue of a service animal in schools is the responsibility for the handling of the animal. This can be a very real concern and one that some administrators have as there are no specific guidelines related to the size and breed of service dogs. However, the law and regulations related to service animals are very clear. First, a service animal must be under the control of its handler. The service animal must have a harness, leash, or other tether, unless:

> The handler is unable, because of a disability, to use a harness, leash, or other tether; or the use of a harness, leash, or other tether would interfere with the service animal's safe, effective performance of work or tasks. In this case, the handler must use voice control, signals, or other effective means to control the service animal. (28 CFR 35.136 (d))

For school district personnel, it is very clear the service animal needs to be under the control of the individual for whom the animal is assigned. If the service animal is assigned to a student, the student must be in control (as noted above) of the animal. If a parent or someone from the community is using a service animal and they are on school property, the individual to whom the service animal is assigned is responsible for the handling of the animal. The rules and guidance we have provided as they relate to schools also applies to other public entities.

SECTION 504

We cover IDEA and the responsibilities of school districts related to service animals in chapter 8. Here we will cover the specifics of Section 504 and service animals. First, we need to clarify what exactly Section 504 is and for whom it is intended.

What Is Section 504?

Section 504 is a brief but powerful nondiscrimination law included in the Rehabilitation Act of 1973. It extended to individuals with disabilities the same kinds of protections Congress extended to people discriminated against because of race and sex. Common disabilities receiving Section 504 Plans in schools include ADHD/ADD, nut allergies, and diabetes. Section 504 states:

> No otherwise qualified individual with a disability . . . shall, solely by reason of his or her disability, be excluded from participating in, be denied the benefits of or be subjected to discrimination under any program or activity receiving Federal financial assistance. (29 U.S.C. § 794(a) [1996])

More important points on Section 504 include:

1. Section 504 is an antidiscrimination law. There are no federal funds provided to school districts for the implementation of this law.
2. The responsibility not to discriminate against individuals with disabilities applies to all school personnel. It is not just students with disabilities who cannot be discriminated against; it is also parents and employees.
3. General education programs and teachers have the primary responsibility for the implementation of Section 504. Staff from special education may be consulted, but they do not have responsibility for implementation of the accommodations for the student.
4. The accommodations required by Section 504 apply to the entire school. This includes parents and visitors to events.

Section 504 and Service Animals

Section 504 of the Rehabilitation Act does not have specifics as a part of the regulations regarding service animals. However, it may require schools (and any other public entity) that receive any form of federal funds, directly or indirectly, to allow a child to bring a service dog to school as a part of the Free Appropriate Public Education (FAPE) requirements of Section 504. It is important to point out that schools do not receive any forms of federal funds to implement the rules and requirements of Section 504; it is solely an antidiscrimination statute. As such, Section 504 of the Rehabilitation Act prohibits disability discrimination in schools. Therefore, if a student (or adult such as a parent) requires the use of a service animal to assist with their disability, the school (or public entity) must make reasonable accommodations to allow this to occur. Enforcement of the rules and regulations of Section 504 are the responsibilities of the Office for Civil Rights (OCR). The OCR has previously determined that a school district violates Section 504 when it does not allow the use of service animals and thus effectively denies a student with disabilities the equal opportunity to participate in or benefit from an educational program.

IDEA AND SERVICE ANIMALS

We cover extensively the rules and regulations related to the Individuals with Disabilities Education Act and service animals in chapter 8. However, since we address the requirements of Section 504 relating to providing the student with a free appropriate public education (FAPE), one of the cornerstones of the IDEA and the services for students eligible for special education and related services, it is important to clarify the components of a FAPE.

How Do I Know If a Service Animal Is Necessary for a FAPE?

A free appropriate public education (FAPE) provides special education and related services that allow an eligible student to make progress toward their goals and objectives. As we note in chapter 8, it is the obligation of school districts to provide a FAPE for students, and this is often done separate from discussions related to service animals. For some students with disabilities, a service dog may be a part of the educational programming for the student. The determination about whether a service animal is necessary for a student is a team decision, and parents are integral members of the team (see chapter 9 for further discussion related to parents). The determination is made after the team clarifies the specific needs of the student and how the school district is going to address those needs. It is based on the needs of the student—not on their disability label nor on what happens to be available within the district. The FAPE determination is a multifaceted one that should include at least the following information:

- the types of tasks the service animal is trained to provide to the student and the extent to which these tasks can be fulfilled by other means (for example, could an aide or school counselor provide some of the services instead of a service animal?);
- the service animal's impact on the student's ability to function successfully and independently;
- the service animal's impact on the student's behavior, including the student's ability to behave appropriately and develop and maintain positive social relationships; and
- whether prolonged separation from the service animal during the school day would affect the student's independent living skills.

CHAPTER 3

EMPLOYEES WITH SERVICE ANIMALS

The regulations of Section 504 as well as guidance from the Department of Justice (see appendix 1) provide that employees and others who come to school (the general public and parents) have the same protections for service animals as students. Emotional support animals and therapy dogs do not have the same protections as those with service animals.

Specifically, the federal regulations state:

(a) General rule
No covered entity shall discriminate against a qualified individual on the basis of disability in regard to job application procedures, the hiring, advancement, or discharge of employees, employee compensation, job training, and other terms, conditions, and privileges of employment (42 U.S.C. 12112).

This rule relates to any employees as long as they are a qualified individual:

(8) Qualified individual
The term "qualified individual" means an individual who, with or without reasonable accommodation, can perform the essential functions of the employment position that such individual holds or desires. For the purposes of this subchapter, consideration shall be given to the employer's judgment as to what functions of a job are essential, and if an employer has prepared a written description before advertising or interviewing applicants for the job, this description shall be considered evidence of the essential functions of the job (42 US Code Section 12111(8)).

For those that are qualified, we need to provide reasonable accommodations:
(9) Reasonable accommodation
The term "reasonable accommodation" may include—
(A) making existing facilities used by employees readily accessible to and usable by individuals with disabilities; and
(B) job restructuring, part-time or modified work schedules, reassignment to a vacant position, acquisition or modification of equipment or devices, appropriate adjustment or modifications of examinations, training materials or policies, the provision of qualified readers or interpreters, and other similar accommodations for individuals with disabilities (42 US Code Section 12111(9)).

Finally, school districts may prevent a service animal from attending school with the employee if the animal, or the accommodations, present an undue hardship.

(10) Undue hardship
(A) In general
The term "undue hardship" means an action requiring significant difficulty or expense, when considered in light of the factors set forth in subparagraph (B).
(B) Factors to be considered
In determining whether an accommodation would impose an undue hardship on a covered entity, factors to be considered include—
(i) the nature and cost of the accommodation needed under this chapter;
(ii) the overall financial resources of the facility or facilities involved in the provision of the reasonable accommodation; the number of persons employed at such facility; the effect on expenses and resources, or the impact otherwise of such accommodation upon the operation of the facility;
(iii) the overall financial resources of the covered entity; the overall size of the business of a covered entity with respect to the number of its employees; the number, type, and location of its facilities; and
(iv) the type of operation or operations of the covered entity, including the composition, structure, and functions of the workforce of such entity; the geographic separateness, administrative, or fiscal relationship of the facility or facilities in question to the covered entity (42 U.S.C. Section 12111(10)).

SUMMARY

The specifics of the difference between a service animal, an emotional support animal, and a psychiatric service animal are very important. Understanding the differences and the language will assist school districts in providing appropriate accommodations for all students and their parents and reduce problems.

CHAPTER 4

TYPES OF SERVICE ANIMALS AND OTHER ASSISTANCE ANIMALS

Dogs have been aiding and working with humans since ancient times, in everything from farming to hunting to protection and more. Service dogs, working dogs, therapy dogs, and emotional support animals all fulfill important roles in their aid to humans, but the terms are not interchangeable. Each recognition is specifically defined, both in terms of the jobs undertaken and the legal rights offered.

—Jan Reisen, American Kennel Club

ADVANCED ORGANIZER

Upon completing this chapter, you will be able to:

- delineate between various types of assistance animals;
- understand the tasks, purpose, and levels of legal protection for each type;
- understand how the Americans with Disabilities Act applies to service animals; and
- understand how the Fair Housing Act and the Air Carrier Act apply to emotional support and service animals.

WE ENCOUNTER ANIMALS in public places more often than ever: at the grocery store, at the laundromat, at the dentist, or perhaps on the city bus or in a taxi. As these occurrences are on the rise in general public spaces, they are also increasingly encountered in school settings.

If you see a vest announcing the animal is working, do you wonder what is its job? Who defines this notion of the dog's *work*? How has the dog been trained? These questions and many more point to the need for a common language and set of definitions. This chapter will explain the types of assistance animals that could be encountered on school campuses.

CHAPTER 4

ASSISTANCE ANIMALS

The benefits of human-animal interaction have been anecdotally supported for many years and increasingly have been empirically documented (Nimer & Lundahl, 2007). Commonly used terms associated with assistance animals could be broadly or specifically defined and easily misunderstood. People who use and/or hear these terms may have varying understanding depending on their prior experiences. Assistance may be described as therapy, support, or service; may be provided by trained professionals; and/or may involve goal-directed activities. The delineation between assistance animals and service animals is not merely determined by the presence of training, formal or otherwise.

An assistance animal provides benefits to an individual and could be a wide variety of animal types (e.g., horse, dog, cat, bird, iguana). Take, for example, pet ownership. The overall health benefits of pet ownership have long been known and now are empirically supported (e.g., Bauman et al., 2020). With pets, however, the benefit is not provided by a trained professional or volunteer working in a therapeutic fashion, and there are no specific goals addressed. Therefore, pets are not considered assistance animals. These delineations help to understand the vocabulary around assistance animals (see table 4.1).

Table 4.1. What Are Characteristics of Different Types of Assistance Animals?

	Service Dog[1]	Psychiatric Service Dog[1]	Alert Dog[1]	Emotional Support Dog/Animal	Therapy Dog/Animal
Specifically trained[2]	✔	✔	✔	S	✔
Performs a specific, disability-related task	✔	✔	✔	X	X
The handler and beneficiary are the same individual	✔	✔	✔	S	X
Defined in ADA	✔	✔[3]	✔[3]	X	X
Defined in FHA	X	X	X	✔[4]	X
Defined in ACA	X	X	X	X	X
Implicated in IDEA	✔	✔	✔	✔	✔
Implicated in ESSA	✔	✔	✔	✔	✔
Implicated in Section 504[5]	✔	✔	✔	✔	✔

Notes: ✔ = yes; X = no; S = sometimes. ADA = Americans with Disabilities Act; FHA = Fair Housing Act; ACA = Air Carrier Act; IDEA = Individuals with Disabilities Act; ESSA = Every Student Succeeds Act.
1. Or miniature horse.
2. Training can be informal or formal.
3. Implicit in service animal definition.
4. Implicit in support animal definition.
5. Section 504 is part of the Rehabilitation Act.

Service Animals

Although this term is often misunderstood and often broadly defined to include other assistance animals, service animals (narrowly defined) have been trained to perform a disability-related task (see table 4.2 and chapter 3). The disability may be a physical or mental impairment and may or may not be readily visible. The only two types of animals considered to be true service animals are dogs and miniature horses. While dogs are the more common type, there are benefits to using miniature horses in service.

The three main benefits of service horses are life span, size, and hair type. While the cost to train a dog and a horse may be similar, the life span of a horse is two to three times longer than a dog, increasing the overall return on investment and decreasing the overall cost of miniature horse training. The life-span benefit also means the individual with a disability will have fewer occurrences of pairing with a new animal. For example, a child with a disability who uses a miniature horse will likely have three or fewer horses in their lifetime whereas

Table 4.2. How Does the Americans with Disabilities Act (ADA, 1990) Define Disability?

Physical impairment	Any physical condition, disfigurement, or loss that affects at least one of these body systems: neurological, musculo-skeletal, special sense organs, respiratory (including speech organs), cardiovascular, reproductive, digestive, genito-urinary, hemic/lymphatic, skin, or endocrine.
Mental impairment	A mental or psychological disorder such as a cognitive impairment, organic brain syndrome, learning disability, or emotional or mental illness.
Physical or mental impairments	Contagious or noncontagious diseases or conditions such as orthopedic, visual, speech, or hearing. Cerebral palsy, epilepsy, muscular dystrophy, multiple sclerosis, cancer, heart disease, diabetes, HIV, tuberculosis, drug addiction, alcoholism. (Physical or mental impairment does not include homosexuality or bisexuality.)
Major life activity	Caring for oneself, performing manual tasks, walking, seeing, hearing, speaking, breathing, learning, and working.
Record of having an impairment	The phrase *has a record of such an impairment* means has a history of, or has been misclassified as having, a mental or physical impairment that substantially limits one or more major life activities.
Regarded as having an impairment	The attitudes of or treatment by other public or private entities as though the individual has a mental or physical impairment.

Disability does not include compulsive gambling, kleptomania, pyromania, transvestism, transsexism, pedophilia, exhibitionism, voyeurism, gender identity not caused by physical impairments, and other sexual behavior disorders. It also does not include psychoactive substance abuse disorders resulting from the current illegal use of drugs.

the same child could have six or more service dogs over the same time period. A miniature horse's size is considered a benefit particularly for individuals with mobility impairments. Because miniature horses are taller, they require less bending and reach from their handler. The larger size of miniature horses allows them to perform tasks that might otherwise be difficult for a dog; for example, providing stability for a taller and/or heavier individual. Another benefit of miniature horses is their hair type; it is less likely to shed and is a viable alternative for individuals with dog allergies.

Service animals may be more specifically identified or categorized by the type of task they are trained to perform that supports their handler with the disability. For example, if a dog is trained to alert its handler of a drop in blood sugar level or is trained to alert of an impending seizure, they may be more specifically called an alert dog. Alert dogs are considered service animals if they meet the same two criteria for other service dogs: (a) trained to perform a specific task, and (b) the task is disability-related. Another example is a psychiatric service dog. These dogs sometimes get confused with emotional support dogs. Again, the clarifying determinant is the specific work the dog has been trained to perform, which is disability-related. For example, veterans who suffer post-traumatic stress may have a service dog trained to establish a physical space separation between the veteran and others in a crowded room or elevator. However, if the dog is *not* trained to do a specific task but provides support by its mere presence, then it would not be considered a service dog—this would be considered a support dog. The determination of a true service animal is always determined by the task (i.e., are they trained to perform a specific task) and by the task mitigating a disability.

Therapy Animals

Therapy animals are not service animals. Instead, they are individually trained for social interaction. Therapy animals are not trained to perform a disability-related task, and the types of animals used in therapy are not limited to a dog or miniature horse as is the case with service animals. While therapy animals do not have the same legal protections under the Americans with Disabilities Act (ADA) as service animals, they may be protected under the Air Carrier Act (ACA) or the Fair Housing Act (FHA) in certain situations (see chapter 3).

Therapy animals have been shown to be beneficial in social and emotional support and to specific populations; for example, individuals with post-traumatic stress, individuals with autism (O'Haire, 2013), young children, senior citizens, emergency room staff and patients (Nahm et al., 2012), and courtroom participants (Spruin et al., 2019). Therapy dogs have been shown to provide physiological benefits such as stress relief (Trammell, 2017); remarkably, the benefit of human-dog interaction has positive physiological responses on the dog as well (Odendaal, 2000).

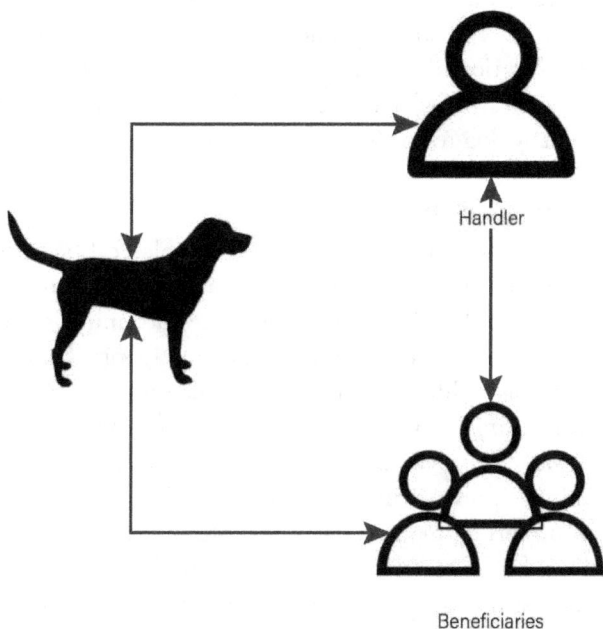

Figure 4.1. Animal Assistance Relationships. *Source:* Kathy Ewoldt

A therapy dog and its handler are certified as a team to provide comfort, stress relief, psychological therapy, and physiological therapy to individuals other than their handlers. Functions of a therapy dog are to be petted by others to relieve stress, promote physical or emotional well-being, or assist with therapy to help an individual meet specific goals. They are considered individually trained pets. They perform tasks for people other than their handlers. As a result, therapy dogs do not have public access with or without their handler. They may only enter buildings that allow pets with a direct invitation to the dog and handler or to the therapy dog organization (Parenti et al., 2013). In some cases, licensed therapists may add therapy dog teams to be part of a specific intervention. These sessions would include specific goals monitored by the therapist.

Characteristics of therapy animals include a reliable disposition and displaying basic obedience skills across environments (MacNamara et al., 2015).

Animal teams are evaluated by organizations to obtain the organization's certification. Animals that enjoy human interaction are best suited as therapy animals. While some types of animals are more likely to be good candidates for formal training, therapy animals come in many shapes and sizes; however, dogs are the most common. Therapy dogs and their handler act as a team, therefore training requires education of both the handler and the dog. Clear communication and rewarding desired behaviors are key features of training that promote the success of therapy dog teams (see chapter 13).

Emotional Support Animals

Although they provide social, emotional, and physiological benefits to people (Tedeschi et al., 2015), emotional support animals are not considered service animals. The increased ubiquity of emotional support animals—and the relative ease to "certify" an animal as an emotional support—has clouded the public's understanding of different types of assistance animals. Broadly defined, emotional support animals may or may not have been trained to perform a specific task; the benefit provided by an emotional support animal simply can arise from the animal's presence in a situation, much like a pet. However, unlike pets, emotional support animals do have legal protections under the FHA and ACA, provided a medical necessity has been established. Some emotional support animals have been trained to perform a specific task to meet a medically diagnosed mental-health disability. In this case, because the animal is trained to perform a disability-related task, they are more narrowly defined as a psychiatric service animal. Psychiatric service animals meet the ADA definition of a service animal.

ASSISTANCE ANIMAL LEGAL PROTECTIONS

Although several disability laws can pertain to service animals (see chapter 3), only three specifically govern service animals. Service animals in the United States have the most legal protection of all therapy and assistance animals. They are protected by the ADA, which defines a service animal as a dog that has been specifically trained to perform a disability-related task. Common misconceptions around service animals are related to certification, training, registration, and identification.

At the national level, there are only two questions that can legally be asked of an individual appearing to use a service animal: (a) Is your animal required due to a disability? and (b) What specific task is your animal trained to perform? Although there are a number of enterprises that have emerged claiming to provide *certification* of service animals, people are often surprised to learn there is no mandate to have a service animal registered as a service animal at the national level. Although several businesses will be glad to take your money and offer you a "certification" and/or "registration," these are not required under ADA.

Additionally, although the animal must be trained to perform disability-related tasks, there is no minimum training requirement or standard. Animals can be self-trained by their handlers or can be formally trained; the only ADA requirement is that they are trained to perform a specific task. An animal that provides benefit from being with a person does not necessarily perform a specific task. People are often surprised to also learn that service animals do not have to wear any identifying paraphernalia such as a vest, harness, leash, or any other marking that identifies the animal as a service animal. However, many individuals who legitimately use a service animal voluntarily choose to have their animal wear an identifying item.

Although there are no national minimums, service animals are required to abide by local ordinances that apply to all animals (e.g., pets) such as state or county licensure and/or immunization requirements. Local veterinarians or county animal control entities can provide stakeholders with information regarding local requirements. Additionally, Michigan State University has created a website describing the nuances of the fifty different state laws at https://www.animallaw.info/topic/table-state-assistance-animal-laws.

Americans with Disabilities Act (ADA)

The Americans with Disabilities Act of 1990 defines service animals as a dog, or in some cases a miniature horse, that has been trained to perform a disability-related task. For the purposes of this discussion, we will limit our term to service dogs to help solidify the narrowness of the definition. The ADA precludes discrimination based on a disability, and it also prevents service animals from being the source of discrimination. An individual with a service dog must be afforded the same opportunities as the general population.

To meet the ADA definition of a service dog, the dog must be trained to perform one or more specific, disability-related tasks for the individual. Dogs must meet the training to perform a specific task requirement and the need to have the task performed must be due to the individual's disability in order to be classified as a true service animal. Disability is defined as a physical or mental impairment that substantially limits at least one of the person's major life activities (49 C.F.R. §37.3; see table 4.2). Major life activities include self-care, "performing manual tasks, walking, seeing, hearing, speaking, breathing, learning, and work" (49 C.F.R. §37.3(2)). There is also a provision of being *regarded* as having an impairment, which means the person is treated generally as having a disability, and having a record of such an impairment. Certain sexual, addictive, and behavior disorders are excluded.

Fair Housing Act (FHA)
In 2020, both the Department of Housing and Urban Development and the Department of Transportation updated their regulations to deter illegitimate claims of support animals by people attempting to gain additional benefit for their pets (e.g., not having to pay a pet deposit, not having to pay pet airline fees). The Fair Housing Act of 1968 requires disability-related animals to be reasonably accommodated, including a waiver of pet fees. Notice that unlike service animals protected by ADA, these animals do not have to perform a disability-related task. Updated FHA regulations use both support animals and service animals in their definitions and limit the allowance for a support/service animal to one per person (Office of Fair Housing and Equal Opportunity, 2020). The allowance of service animals for residents is typically clear cut. However, support animals may cause some confusion.

Prior to the 2020 updated regulation, it was fairly easy for residents to pay a fee to online providers and get a letter from a medical professional stating the animal was a necessary emotional support. However, recent updates are helping to limit claims of emotional support animals to individuals who have a legitimate disability and need for the animal. The types of animals protected under the FHA are those animals typically found in homes such as dogs, cats, small birds, rabbits, hamsters, gerbils, other rodents, fish, or turtles. Animals not typically kept in homes, such as monkeys, kangaroos, and chickens, may also be accommodated if the individual can substantially justify the need for the animal to provide support. The justification must include documentation from a health-care professional confirming the disability-related need. Support animals do not have to be specifically trained; they can provide benefit merely from their presence. They are differentiated from a pet in their disability-related need for such benefit.

Air Carrier Access Act
Like the FHA, the Air Carrier Access Act of 1986 (ACA) was amended in 2020. The ACA previously used the term "emotional support animals" but now limits animals to the more narrow definition of a service dog. Under the ACA, emotional support animals are now treated as pets. However, it may be helpful

to note the delineation in the ACA between an emotional support animal and a psychiatric service animal. If the dog is trained to perform a disability-related task, it is a psychiatric service dog. If the dog provides disability-related benefits by its presence, it is an emotional support. Unlike service dog protections provided by the ADA, the ACA is allowed to require documentation of the dog's health, behavior, and training.

Other Considerations
Conversations with individuals who have an animal are sometimes difficult to navigate. Disabilities may or may not be readily obvious. With clearly visible disabilities, such as mobility and some autism-related disabilities, it is a generally straightforward determination that the animal is providing a disability-related service. However, in the case of less obvious disabilities, particularly when animals provide emotional-related services, more conversation is required in making the determination if the animal is fulfilling a disability-related need. When these conversations occur, there is protection of privacy for the individuals; they are never required to disclose or identify their disability, although some may choose to do so. There are only two questions that can be asked legally (see "Assistance Animal Legal Protections" above).

In all cases, the animal must be under the control of the handler and must be housebroken. If an animal becomes unruly, the handler must take action to regain control. Also, animals must be capable of eliminating in designated areas. This control can be verbal. The law specifically states that service animals do not need to be on a leash if the leash inhibits the animal's ability to perform its disability-related work.

We have discussed different types of assistance animals used in service, interventions, and therapy. There are also some instances where a dog is considered to be in a dual role when there are expectations for the dog to perform different types of assistance in certain situations.

In the classroom, there may be temptation on the part of teachers or leadership to see a service dog as capable of also providing a specified benefit to other students in the classroom equivalent to that of a therapy animal. While there will likely be collateral benefits to other students, similar to having pets, placing additional duties or responsibilities on a service animal has consequences. Dual-role animals can become more easily fatigued and may be confused by the expected differing behaviors that would be situationally dependent, and this dual-role practice may be viewed as unethical. For example, Therapy Dogs International will not certify a service dog as a therapy dog.

SUMMARY

There are a wide variety of animal types that provide differing assistance to people. These animals may or may not be domesticated, and the assistance may or may not be related to an ADA-defined disability. When an assistance animal is trained to perform a specific, disability-related task, it is defined as a service animal and is protected under ADA. The ADA has the narrowest definition of what constitutes a service animal, whereas the FHA and ACA are more liberal in their approaches. Unfortunately, the various definitions assigned to different types of animals lead to discrepancies in terminology usage among the general public and between different animal organizations. In the classroom, assistance animals may or may not be legally protected.

For more information, see the Alliance of Therapy Dog Training (https://www.therapydogs.com/puppy-therapy-dog-training/) and Pet Partners (https://petpartners.org/).

CHAPTER 5

SERVICE ANIMAL TRAINING AND ACQUISITION

He is a total part of my family though caring for him can feel like as much work as parenting. . . . The challenges—and rewards—are all worth considering if you're contemplating a service dog of your own.

—Cindy Kuzma, "Everything You Need to Know before Getting a Service Dog"

ADVANCED ORGANIZER

After reading this chapter, you will be able to:

- determine questions to ask before seeking a service animal,
- identify types of service animals,
- understand specific jobs service animals can perform,
- recognize possible problems and concerns to address,
- gain knowledge of service animal training as an industry,
- understand training requirements and various stages involved in training, and
- access resources and recommendations for finding reputable training.

WITHIN THIS CHAPTER, we will discuss the process and questions one must consider in the acquisition of a service animal. The use of a service animal is a decision that should not be taken lightly, as it has long-term ramifications not only for the animal but for the individual who may require the service the animal provides. Additionally, when one fraudulently makes use of an effective service animal, it denies the use of the animal to someone who may sincerely require its assistance. As repeatedly noted in other chapters, there are unscrupulous individuals who may not truly have the service animal's interest as a foremost thought when they charge for their services, and we encourage the reader to be cautious. Finally, not all service animals have to receive professional training, as there is no state or national requirement for such. There are ways that individuals could train their own service animal for the specific roles and responsibilities that are needed. In the following section, considerations involved in each step of acquiring a service animal are presented and addressed.

QUESTIONS TO ASK

A service animal may be one of the biggest financial investments an individual makes, and it may also be one of the most important in improving the life of an individual with a disability. It can also foster a level of independence that was not previously available and create opportunities that were previously not considered.

Question 1: Why?

First, why a service animal? In order to acquire a service animal, a person must have a disability as defined by the Americans with Disabilities Act and need the support of the animal to mitigate the impact of the disability. Service animals are not provided to individuals just so they have a pet. There needs to be a clear reason and need for the use of the animal based on the person's disability. The typical reasons why an individual may need a service animal may include problems related to scoliosis or physical problems, a seizure disorder, vision loss, hearing loss, autism, PTSD (though see the section on emotional support animals below), and multiple sclerosis. This is not a definitive list but provides broad parameters.

Having a disability does not automatically qualify or entitle someone to get a service animal. It is not as if someone loses their vision and they immediately get an animal. Both personal and disability-related factors should be considered. For example, there are some individuals who do not like animals, or there may be a form of technology that the individual would rather use or could do the job better than a service animal. Additionally, each and every disability is individual to the person, with no two people responding to the disability in the same way or with the same needs. Therefore, we need to make sure the person is treated as an individual and not make assumptions about their disability or their needs.

The severity of the disability is also a driving force behind the consideration for the service animal. Some individuals with hearing loss are independent and do not have needs that can be addressed by a service animal. Other individuals who are deaf or hard of hearing believe that a service animal would provide a great deal of assistance and be a benefit to their lives in many ways. The same is true for all the above listed disabilities.

Question 2: Why? Part 2

Why the need for a service animal? Yes, it is a given as listed above that the person must have a disability. However, beyond that, what are the specific tasks a service animal may provide that would be of assistance? This question is a reminder that service animals are different from emotional support animals, and just desiring the comfort or companionship of an animal is not enough to warrant the need or use of a service animal. There are many different tasks that a service animal may perform, and the following examples are taken from the Americans with Disabilities Act 2010 guidance on service animals.

> Examples of such work or tasks include guiding people who are blind, alerting people who are deaf, pulling a wheelchair, alerting and protecting a person who is having a seizure, reminding a person with mental illness to take prescribed medications, calming a person with Post Traumatic Stress Disorder (PTSD) during an anxiety attack, or performing other duties. Service animals are working animals, not pets. The work or task a dog has been trained to provide must be directly related to the person's disability. Dogs whose sole function is to provide comfort or emotional support do not qualify as service animals under the ADA. (U.S. Department of Justice, 2011)

Question 3: How?

How will the animal be cared for? Service animals are highly trained for the role they are expected to play in the individual's life (as listed above). However, they still need to be cared for and provided multiple opportunities a day to relieve themselves. A service dog will almost always live with their owner, so the house should be clean, safe, and physically animal-friendly. Service animals can live in any building regardless of no-pet rules, but they still need regular and frequent access to the outdoors.

If you are seeking a service dog, what type of breed would be better for the needs that are to be addressed? This is a very important question that depends on the answer of why a service animal is needed. Many of the tasks that a service animal must perform are physical in nature. Therefore, the need(s) dictate the type of dog, not the other way around. For example, if the service dog is needed to prompt an individual with a seizure disorder, that is a very different need than if the service dog is needed to help support the individual as they are walking or standing. Other service animals are used to obtain objects from high places, pick things up off the floor, assist with pushing big loads, alert to certain sounds, or assist an individual with a visual impairment to maneuver through traffic or sidewalks. The responsibilities and tasks that a service animal performs are varied. The nature of the task helps dictate the appropriate breed. Finally, not all dogs can work as a service animal. Even if the dog is the right size for the job and can perform the necessary task(s), the temperament of the dog needs to be addressed. There needs to be an unflappable temperament and a degree of trainability along with support for the individual. All of this needs to be taken into consideration when determining the right dog for the job.

There are some individuals with disabilities who choose to use horses as their service animal. When one thinks of a horse, the usual thought is of one that is over six feet tall. However, ADA allows the use of miniature horses as service animals. Miniature horse typically weigh between seventy to ninety pounds and are only about three to four feet tall. Again, we need to ask the question: what is the service animal expected to perform? If the answer is to serve as a stability force when walking, a service horse might be the right choice. Miniature horses are of a size to support someone with a disability that impairs their mobility. Their height is close to the hip height of many individuals, and the horses have a strong, well-built body; as a result, a service horse might be ideal for someone who might lose their balance.

Additionally, when thinking of the dog breed that might be used, there are some individuals that are allergic to different types of dog hair. This would rule out the use of many breeds of dogs that are typically used as service animals. Miniature horses, on the other hand, can be easier to groom and do not shed or trigger allergies like dogs can, and they do not get fleas. A service horse would be more suited to someone who is very sensitive to hair and has severe allergies.

Question 4: Space?

Do you have the space and housing appropriate for a service animal, be it a dog or a horse? Will there be opportunities for the animal to go outside, or do you live in a housing complex that makes getting from where you live to outside difficult? Do you have space for the animal to have a safe place to sleep and rest when they are not working? Do you have space for the food and other supplies they may require?

Question 5: Other Animals?

Are there other animals in the living situation or nearby that may cause problems? This continues the question above about the safety and security of the service animal. If the service animal is threatened—or feels threatened—the ability for them to adequately and appropriately do their job will be impaired. You may have a safe environment within your living space, but is it safe for the animal once they venture out with you?

Question 6: Others for Advice?

Is there someone in a similar situation (or with a similar disability) with a service animal you can talk with? Service animals can be a huge asset to the person with a disability. However, they are also real live animals that may take some work during the course of every day. Talk with others who have had service animals, and when discussing the options, make sure to address the positives of having a service animal but also the negatives. Be very specific about your needs and how they are to be addressed, and work to obtain candid remarks about the pros and cons. Also, try to obtain examples and stories from others about surprises and disappointments. As addressed multiple times throughout this book, a service animal may be one of the best investments (see costs below) that can be made to improve the life and independence of a person with a disability. However, service animals may not necessarily be the perfect solution for every individual, and having an animal around may be more work than benefit. Finally, there are some people who just do not like (or are fearful of) dogs (or small horses).

Question 7: Finances?

Before we address the cost of obtaining a qualified service animal and contacting agencies that either provide service animals or assistance with the acquisition costs, it is important to address the annual costs of the upkeep of the animal. Unlike a piece of technology that may have a onetime cost, service animals need a variety of supports throughout the years in order for them to be able to effectively perform their job.

The following are very rough estimates of the costs of having a service animal over a year. There may be other factors to consider, but these are ones that are likely to be a part of every service animal's life. There may also be cheaper methods of providing these services; however, it is important to keep in mind the service animal must have their needs addressed so they can work. Again, the following are the basics that should reasonably be expected. One can always spend more on their animals through buying them expensive treats or toys. Sometimes it is difficult to not want to purchase items that will make their lives better.

Table 5.1. Annual Costs of Having a Service Animal

Item	Annual Cost
Veterinarian care	$300
Food	$450
Flea and tick medication	$240
Heartworm medication	$110
Insurance	$275
Annual Total	**$1,375**

There are organizations that may provide financial assistance to individuals in need. However, it is important to understand that there are costs associated with the regular and necessary upkeep of a service animal over a year. The costs listed above are for a service dog. A service horse would also have costs. However, there are differences in that service horses do not get fleas.

Question 8: Finances? Part 2
The first part of the finance question dealt with the reality of whether a service animal could be afforded once they were obtained. Yes, there are organizations that support individuals with service animals; however, the point of the question was to ensure appropriate consideration of the costs and supports needed for a successful service animal experience. The next part of the question is the actual cost of obtaining a service animal.

There are many different programs that train service animals. Before discussing costs, the reader is encouraged to read the chapter on training a service animal. The training is very important as the needs of the individual with a disability may be very specific and the settings and situations where the services are needed may change over time and the animal will need to adapt and be ready for these new situations. Additionally, as a part of the training, the animal will need to be trained in a firm but gentle manner that focuses on positive reinforcement, allowing the animal to not be fearful or scared of others or the handlers.

The costs of a well-trained service animal can range from $5,000 to $40,000. It depends on the animal, the skills that have been taught, the length of the training, and the amount of follow-through that will be provided after the initial match with the individual with a disability. There are some organizations that match the animal with the person and then provide very little (if any) supports afterward to ensure the match and pairing is one that is working for the individual with a disability and for the animal. There needs to be follow-up—more than a cursory phone call—that ensures the match is working, addressing the needs, and not making life worse for either the person with a disability or the animal.

Questions to ask of the agency training the service animal include: What is the animal actually being trained to perform? What are expectations for reinforcement for the tasks? When will there be retraining, if any? Whom do you contact if there are problems? Are there needs for additional services or skills? How many animals have they trained in the past? What is the success rate of those animals? How do they define success? Can you talk to individuals who have received animals from them in the past?

Before we fully address the cost of obtaining a service animal, we need to point out that one does not need to purchase a service animal and that the animal can be trained "in house." However, we need to remind the reader of the differences between a service animal and an emotional support animal. Many pets provide comforting or emotional support services to their respective owners, but a service animal is an animal that provides not just emotional comfort to the individual but also provides service and assists with specific tasks related to their disability. For a greater explanation of the differences between a service animal and an emotional support animal, the reader is referred to chapter 3.

Self-training. Self-training a service animal can potentially save a lot of money and time needed in the acquisition of an animal; however, it is not a task that should be undertaken lightly. A service animal often needs extensive socialization training, extensive training on the specific tasks they will be expected to perform, and, for some, extensive training on dealing with waiting around while their handler is at work, class, or meetings.

Specifically, as a part of any training for a service animal, whatever animal is used, there are several items that need to be addressed as a part of the training. The following components will also help in the determination about whether a particular animal can work as a service animal. The following points also will help the reader understand that not all pet dogs or miniature horses can become a service animal. There is clearly a temperament that is necessary to support the person in need. Some of the following points can be addressed through socialization and training, but there are some that may be difficult to obtain through training alone.

First, any service animal should be trained to be calm in settings in which they are unfamiliar. This is important because their responsibilities are for the individual in need, and as the locations change, the responsibilities to the person do not. The tasks may change depending on the situation; however, it is important for the animal to remain calm. For dogs, this may affect the breeds that are chosen to work with the individual. Temperament of specific dogs should be considered as well. Overall, certain breeds are better suited to service work because of their function, but the temperament of the individual dog must be assessed.

Second, service animals need to be trained to be alert to the needs of the individual. They are to provide the necessary supports and tasks for that one individual. That is their job. Reacting to others and not paying attention to the needs of the individual will pose problems and prevent the animal from performing their job and helping the individual.

Third, service animals need to be able to please the individual with a disability and get their reinforcement from doing so. The animal may go a long time without typical reinforcement of a treat or being told that what they are doing is good, and they will need to have been weaned from the requirement of continuous reinforcement to intermittent reinforcement for successful completion of a task. This takes time and a level of consistency, along with understanding intermittent reinforcement as opposed to specific schedules of reinforcement.

Fourth, the animal needs to be able to be trained. This means it can learn new tasks and be able to transfer that information to novel situations. Additionally, the animal should be able to retain information from previous experiences and settings that will assist the individual with a disability. Not all animals can do this, but this is an important skill for the long-term care of the individual.

Fifth, as a part of the training, the animal will require extensive socialization experiences. The animal should be exposed to many different types of situations involving not only other people but other animals as well. The situations need to have noise, congestion, crowds, flashing lights, darkness, unusual smells, smells from food, sirens, and other animals. This, like the other steps listed above, takes a concerted effort and will take time. As a part of the socialization experiences for animals prior to their specific service animal training, the individuals working with the animals are encouraged to take the animals everywhere because the unpredictability of what they will experience is very good for the long-term socialization of the animal.

Sixth, as a part of the training, the animal should be one that can be trusted to perform the required tasks. This means, like other points above, that the animal should be able to ignore other demands or possible exciting activities going on around them and focus on the needs of the individual with a disability. For some animals, this is going to be very difficult and will require extensive training. This also should be a reason to focus on a dog that has matured and not just a young dog who has not shown that it can pay attention or ignore other items or activities.

Seventh, the animal will need to be able to demonstrate that it can not only ignore the other activities around it but also reliably do the same activities over and over again. The needs of the individuals with disabilities may be very repetitive (e.g., picking things up off the ground, reminders for alarms, or being there to be leaned upon). The animal needs to be able and willing to do the same tasks over and over.

Finally, the training of a service animal is not something that should be taken lightly. The requirements for a service animal are that the animal is required because of a disability and that the animal is specifically trained to perform tasks that assist the individual. These requirements are obviously different than those for an emotional support animal. These questions above apply to animals that are trained locally or in house and for service animals that are purchased or acquired from other agencies (see below).

Question 9: Finances? Part 3

What is the actual cost? The actual cost of a service animal can vary from a few thousand dollars to close to fifteen to twenty thousand dollars. Many individuals who have service animals talk about it as a great investment in the level of independence that is provided to the person with a disability. It is hard to put a price on someone's independence, but the reality is that many people do not have extra money to spend on a service animal.

There are many organizations that assist with the payment, either as a grant or as a long-term loan to help pay for the initial costs of a service animal. As noted above, if the organizations can assist in providing financial assistance in obtaining a qualified animal, then one can get an animal of a breed that is likely to be of the most assistance. This does cost, but the costs are spread out over time, making it more palatable than the initial onetime cost for purchasing a service animal.

Finally, before we talk about the decisions that must be made in actually obtaining a service animal, the costs of obtaining an animal can be tax deductible. One still has to spend the money obtaining the animal, and then a percentage of that will be returned when there is a reconciliation of the taxes.

LACK OF REGULATION

A service animal can be a great asset to an individual in need of assistance. Also, as we have noted above, one can train their own service animal. As is pointed out in other parts of this book, there are ways anyone can purchase a service animal vest for an animal and claim the benefits of taking an animal to wherever it is needed. There are very few regulations about what constitutes a service animal, and there are also very few regulations about how much or what kind of training is necessary for an animal to become a service animal.

Given that there are very few (if any) regulations about what is necessary for the training of a service animal, it makes it difficult to choose a reputable provider when making a purchase of what could be a very expensive—and personal—item. In addition to the list of questions above, the following questions will help when making a decision about how and where to choose a provider of a service animal. As the reader can see, the questions in this chapter address the seriousness of the nature of working with a service animal. It is not a decision that should be undertaken lightly, and if there is not proper training, there could be long-term negative consequences for the individual with a disability, for their family, and also for the animal itself.

QUESTIONS TO ASK OF THE TRAINER

1. What is their background?
2. How long have they been training service animals?
3. How many service animals have they trained?
4. How do they provide instruction to the animals?
5. How long do they work with the animals before they are placed?
6. How many animals have they placed?
7. What are the steps they do to pair the individual with a disability and the animal?
8. How long is the pairing process?
9. What guidance do they give the individual with a disability?
10. Do they visit the individual with a disability at home/work/other to assist in determining what is needed?
11. What are the steps for long-term working with the animal?
12. What follow-up steps do they engage in after the animal is placed?
13. What certifications do they hold?
14. Can you talk with individuals who have had animals placed with them?
15. What do their critics say about them?
16. How many animals do they take back after determining that the match is not a good one?
17. Will they provide another animal if the initial match is not a good one?
18. What is their refund policy?
19. Do they have guidance about what to do the first day home with the animal? Second day? First week?

Finally, if possible, ask about the genetics and history of the parents of the possible service animal. If there is the possibility, meet the service animal's parents. Check their temperament and personalities as well as their physical traits. Clarify whether the animals have been checked for any genetic disorders that may affect the service animal's health later in life. Additionally, ask if there is a return policy. Some animals and handlers are not right for each other, and there may need to be another attempt at addressing these needs.

As you can see, you must be careful in making a determination about the need for a service animal. If you can, go with a reputable trainer who has a long-term history of success in providing service animals to individuals with disabilities. There is no government-sanctioned certification, and as noted above, one can train their own service animal.

The most important thing is the long-term support involved. Will the organization that has trained the animal commit to the time necessary to continue the work? Will they ensure the match is good by training the handler or person with a disability?

TRAINING FOR THE HANDLER OR PERSON WITH A DISABILITY

We have spent a lot of time focused on the training of the animal. This is very important, but just as important is the training necessary for the handler or person with a disability. One cannot just assume that the service animal and the handler will work together and everything will be a success. The following are guidelines and questions that need to be addressed.

First, many service animal organizations expect the individual to be at least fourteen years of age. Undoubtedly there are individuals under this age who have a service animal, but the focus is on the age/maturity necessary to control an animal in unpredictable situations.

Second, the handler of the service animal[1] must be physically capable of participating in a training process for at least an hour a day to familiarize them with the animal. They must complete the requisite training in how to use the skills that the animal has acquired.

Third, the handler of the animal must be cognitively capable of understanding the commands, the responsibilities, and the necessary steps for care of the animal. This includes the ability to fully understand the roles and responsibilities the animal may play in the life of a person with a disability but also when interacting in society.

Fourth, the handler needs to be able to command and handle the service animal. They need to be able to do this independently of any other individual.

---

1. For the purposes of this discussion, we will use the term *handler* to refer to both the person with a disability who will be using the animal and any other person who may be working as a handler for the animal. There is a difference, but this is done for clarity's sake. The information for a handler, whether it is the person with a disability or not, is the same information.

Without the ability to command the service animal, there will be potentially severe problems with the match and the service that is expected to be provided.

Fifth, as has been noted throughout this book, meeting the needs of the person with a disability is very important. But, in order for this to occur, the needs of the animal also are to be addressed. Therefore, the handler needs to be able to meet the physical needs as well as the emotional needs of the animal. The animal may need a place to exercise on a regular basis and the opportunity to not be "at work" or "on call" twenty-four hours a day.

Sixth, the handler needs to be able to meet the financial needs of the animal. This includes the basics like food and a warm, quiet place to sleep but also the needs related to veterinarian care and any medicines or vaccines that are required.

Seventh, the handler needs to live in a stable home environment. There needs to be consistency in where the animal will sleep, where they will be expected to work, and with whom they are expected to interact.

Eighth, the handler can have other animals, but there is an expectation by some agencies for service dogs that there will be no other dogs in the household. Not having other dogs (and limited animals) provides an easier opportunity to the service animal to perform their jobs and responsibilities without unneeded distraction.

Ninth, the handler has to commit to actively working to ensure the service animal is respected and treated with dignity throughout their stay, no matter where they are required to work. This can take on many forms, but in essence, the handler needs to be an advocate for the service animal and actively work to ensure their well-being.

Requalification Requirements

There are some organizations that periodically require the individual with a disability using a service animal to become requalified to receive assistance. The typical thought behind this step is to ensure the animals are provided to those who are in need, not just those who want, as the animals are designed to work and have received many hours of training. Providing documentation of need is typically all that is required. This may involve a note from one's physician, physical therapist, or occupational therapist. If an organization that places animals has this as a requirement, it important to take this step seriously. First, the service animal may truly be providing assistance to the person with a disability. Second, in many instances, the service animal becomes close to the person and to the rest of the family as well. It may be difficult to part as a result of this closeness. Third, as noted above, the service animal has been trained to provide assistance to a person with a disability. If the animal is not needed or not being used appropriately, it would be better to provide assistance to an individual who really needs help.

Introduction and Transition

It would be great if every animal trained was a perfect match for the person with a disability. However, that is not always the case. We have covered the questions that should be addressed prior to choosing whether a service animal is needed or even appropriate. The next step, after the decision that a service animal is needed, is to find a reputable agency or organization that trains service animals.

Living with a Service Animal

After a service animal has been provided, there will be some adjustment to having an animal in the household. There are some very important components that need to be addressed and should not be forgotten. The following section discusses the needs of the animal that are to be addressed, which include work, play, rest, and training. As one can see from the contents of this chapter, acquiring a service animal is a decision that should not be taken lightly. Additionally, it may seem like a long process with lots to consider in making a determination about a service animal, but the real work comes after there is a match and the service animal is in place at the home. That is where the real work begins, and it does not end.

Work. The main reason for a service animal is the work they will provide to the person with a disability. As noted above, if there is no need for the service animal, then it would make sense to provide a well-trained animal to another individual to assist with their needs. Some animals are working all day from early in the day until the end. Others are only needed intermittently, and their responsibilities may not start until later in the day or may only be necessary when out among the public or moving to and from places of work.

Training. Before an animal becomes a service animal, it undergoes extensive training. This training is necessary to determine first if the animal can perform the tasks that are required for the job but also to ensure they have the temperament to be a successful service animal. This training provides a solid foundation. However, the training does not stop once the animal is matched and placed. There needs to be consistent training after the placement to ensure the skills are maintained and necessary new skills are refined and mastered. Therefore, training must continue, and the training must be consistent so that the animal learns the necessary skills.

Play. All animals will require an opportunity to have time where they are not working. Typically, we think of this time as play time. Whether the animal actually engages in play with a person or with another animal is not the point. The animal needs an opportunity to not be working all the time. As long as the animal receives adequate and consistent training, it does not need to be working all the time. Play also allows the animal to interact with others in different ways.

Relaxation. Some service animals are working from early in the morning to late at night. The wide variety of jobs and responsibilities that animals have is truly remarkable. However, relaxation for the animal is important, and it should be provided to reduce the long-term stress an animal may experience.

Rest. In order to do their job effectively, service animals will need a lot of rest. This is different from relaxation above. This is not just time not working but time that allows the animal to sleep and have no demands placed upon them. It does not necessarily have to be all at one time; however, the rest/sleep afforded at night is very important. There are some service animals that are expected to work at night, alerting the handler to a seizure, awakening an individual with PTSD from a bad dream, or assisting with getting the individual to and from the bathroom. Work to schedule specific time that allows for relaxation (listed above) and rest where the service animal may recharge and then be able to perform the necessary tasks for which they are expected. Not being provided adequate or appropriate rest can exacerbate health issues the animal may have or in the long term may even shorten the animal's life, as dogs traditionally require twelve to fourteen hours of sleep per day.

Accreditation

As you see in this chapter and the rest of this book, there is no federal certification for what animal becomes a service animal. We have even discussed self-training an animal and the necessary work that is involved in that process. The vast majority of individuals seeking to obtain a service animal use an organization known for training the animals. This is not an endorsement, as the field of service animal training has a long way to go; however, strongly consider using an accredited organization when thinking about obtaining a service animal. There is one resource that is working to facilitate users in obtaining a trained service animal, Assistance Dog International (https://assistancedoginternational.org).

Having accreditation means they have worked through the various steps necessary to document their efforts to others and demonstrated that they are following procedures, have a history of providing services, and hold themselves accountable to others. As we have noted, there are no federal guidelines on the training of a service animal, and individuals could do this themselves. There are also other organizations providing accreditation.

Actual Places

Depending on your location and need for a service animal, there are different organizations providing support and awareness on this. Again, we are not endorsing one organization over another, and we strongly encourage the use of an organization that has a long-term history of providing service animals and is willing to obtain accreditation and abide by standards of care, support, and transition.

SUMMARY

As you can see, there are a lot of questions that need to be addressed prior to placing a service animal with a person with a disability. It is not a decision to be taken lightly. However, it is a decision that can have a long-term benefit for the person and facilitate their independence.

CHAPTER 6

SERVICE ANIMALS IN SCHOOLS

Schools are a microcosm of society. Individuals from the community with and without disabilities enter the school building for educational, recreational, and civic activities and bring with them these various types of service dogs. As a result, school personnel are often confronted with the task of determining the extent of access a service dog and handler have to school buildings in general and the classrooms in particular.

—Anne O. Papalia, "Service Dogs in Schools"

ADVANCED ORGANIZER

Upon completing this chapter, you will be able to:

- outline a framework for determining the access afforded to support and service animals in schools;
- identify legal and educational factors involved in determining access;
- describe strategic handling skills involved in using a service animal in schools, including ramifications for specific areas in the school (e.g., cafeteria, public areas, classroom, nurse's office, restrooms, therapy rooms, science labs, etc.);
- discuss strategies and implications for the interaction of service animals with other animals in the school setting; and
- recognize the importance of educating other students, faculty, and staff on service animal etiquette.

"I'M SORRY, NO PETS ARE ALLOWED IN SCHOOLS." "Is this a service animal?" "How does that miniature horse help you with your disability?" "You'll need to show me before you can enter the classroom." "That dog will be too distracting to be in the classroom. The children will never be able to learn with it in the class." "What about the students with allergies in her class? It's not fair to them." Handlers, both children and adults, encounter these and many other statements when they enter a school building with their service animals.

Schools by nature are a gathering place for the community. Community members with and without disabilities enter schools for educational, recreational, and civic activities. The use of service animals, support animals, and therapy animals has expanded as well. Schools are often confronted with the task of determining if a service animal and its handler can enter the school building in general and the classroom in particular. Multiple factors must be considered, including the nature of support the dog provides, the dog's training and certification, and the legal protections afforded to the service animal and handler (Papalia, 2018). Consider the following scenarios. Results of the scenarios are presented later in the chapter.

Moses and Orient

Moses is a fourth grader with a physical disability who uses a wheelchair. His parents are requesting that Moses's service animal accompany him while he is in school. His miniature horse named Orient performs tasks such as helping Moses balance while transferring to and from his chair and pulling the wheelchair up ramps when Moses is not able to climb them on his own. Mrs. Sellers, Moses's teacher, is concerned about Orient joining the class because one student in her class is allergic to horses and a speech therapist who visits the classroom is afraid of horses. Can Orient attend school with Moses? Why or why not?

Ming Lee and Elsie

Ming Lee is a tenth grader who experiences test anxiety. Her counselor recommended that Ming Lee bring her emotional support dog to school when Ming Lee takes tests. The dog, a Shih Tzu named Elsie, has lived with Ming Lee's family for the past three years. Ming Lee's parents noted she tends to experience less anxiety when she holds Elsie in her lap. Can Elsie come to school on test days? Why or why not?

Mr. Davidson and Radar

Mr. Davidson has two children enrolled in Mayfair Elementary School. He is coming to the school to drop off his daughter's lunch to the kindergarten classroom. Mr. Davidson has a specially trained psychiatric service dog that assists him due to PTSD. Mr. Davidson is in the school office and wants to bring his daughter's lunch directly to her classroom. The school secretary says that he must leave the lunch with her and cannot go to the classroom. Mr. Davidson becomes upset because he feels he is being denied access to the classroom because of his service dog, a rottweiler/Labrador retriever mix named Radar. Can Mr. Davidson bring his dog to the classroom? Why or why not?

Mrs. Rohena and Bright

Mrs. Rohena has diabetes and uses a diabetic alert dog named Bright. She is attending a high school musical, *Into the Woods*, to see her daughter perform. School personnel question her about bringing the dog in school and ask about the nature of her disability. Can Mrs. Rohena bring Bright to school? Why or why not?

Rosemary and Solomon

Rosemary volunteers at State Street Elementary School with her therapy dog, Solomon. The first graders read to the dog. Solomon is certified as a therapy dog by Therapy Dog International. A parent of a student in the class has complained to the first-grade teacher about the therapy dog visits because her son is allergic to dogs. Rosemary indicates to the teacher that Solomon can continue to visit the class regardless of allergies because he is a certified therapy dog and is entitled to rights under ADA. Can Solomon continue to visit the class? Why or why not?

Jonas and Jinx

Jonas Scepter is a second-grade boy with autism who receives special education services. His IEP states he can bring his service dog, Jinx, to school. Jinx is a two-year-old golden retriever that recently completed service dog training. During the first few visits, Jinx was unruly in the classroom. He barked excessively, startling students and interrupting instruction. Jinx pulled away from Jonas on several occasions and ran from the classroom into the hall. Jinx also ate a part of another student's lunch while in the cafeteria. The principal asked Jonas's mother to keep Jinx at home. She refuses, indicating the school is violating ADA by not allowing Jonas to bring Jinx in school because a provision for using a service dog is in Jonas's IEP. Can Jinx come to school? Why or why not?

The answers to these scenarios depend upon several factors: (a) if the animal is qualified for designation as a service animal based upon the tasks it performs for the handler and the training the animal has received, (b) the person's role in the school, and (c) the legal protection offered within each circumstance.

The purpose of this chapter is to provide a framework for determining access to various types of support animals into schools and to present strategic handling elements that will support their continued use. The framework for determining access is based on the legal status of the service animal, the role of the handler, and the nature of service provided by the animal. Examples of strategic handling factors include educating school personnel and other students on legalities of service animals' use, knowledge and implementation of service dog etiquette, and collaborative addressing of contextual issues within the classroom and school at large.

The chapter focuses primarily on service dogs because canines are the species directly recognized in the Americans with Disabilities Act (ADA) as a service animal. In specific cases, ADA also recognizes miniature horses as service animals. Information regarding miniature horses is provided in specific context as well. Vocabulary and titles are important when discussing service and support animals because each term implies a specific level of access and legal protection. The term *service dog* or *service animal* is used within this chapter to identify animals meeting the ADA criteria. The term *support dogs/animals* is used as a generic term to identify animals working for the benefit of people that do not meet the ADA definition. A discussion of specific types of service dogs and support animals is provided in chapter 1.

FRAMEWORK FOR DETERMINING SERVICE ANIMAL ACCESS

A three-step framework can be used to determine service animal access within a school. The first step is to determine if the animal meets the definition of a service animal under the ADA. Next, the role of the handler and the nature of the visit must be considered. Last, the nature of the support the animal provides in terms of assistance and educational benefits must be clarified to determine if the animal and handler are protected under civil rights legislation (the ADA), educational legislation (Individuals with Disabilities Education Act), or both (Papalia, 2018).

Step 1: Determining Service Dog Status

The first step in determining the extent of school access for a service animal is to determine if the animal meets the ADA service definition. Service animal designation is based upon the function the animal performs for the person with a disability and the nature of training the dog has received. According to the ADA, a service animal must be individually trained to perform tasks for the benefit of an individual with a disability that he or she could not perform for him- or herself and that make the disability less severe, serious, or painful. The courts have identified three criteria for defining a service animal. It must (a) be specially trained and not merely exhibiting a natural behavior, (b) mitigate the person's disability, and (c) be needed by the specific handler (US Department of Justice, 2011).

When determining if an animal is a service animal as defined by ADA, school personnel can only ask specific types of questions. They can inquire if the animal is a service animal required because of a disability and the type of work or task the dog has been trained to perform. School personnel cannot ask for disability-related information such as the nature of the person's disability or requiring medical documentation. Neither can they request the animal demonstrate its ability to perform the work or task it is trained to do (US Department of Justice, 2011).

The limited nature of these inquiries make it difficult to determine if an animal meets ADA requirements, especially in cases when the handler has an invisible disability. Another confounding factor revolves around the increased use of support dogs and expanding titles given to service dogs. It can be difficult to decipher the ADA status by the animal's title. The following section contains a brief overview of various types of support and service dogs to help clarify their status.

Psychiatric service animals. Psychiatric service dogs are a specific type of service animal individually trained to mitigate their handler's psychiatric disability. They are used by a person with a psychiatric impairment limiting one or more life functions stated in the ADA definition of disability (e.g., learning, reading, concentrating, thinking, communicating, and sleeping). Only individuals who are actually disabled by a psychiatric impairment qualify to use a psychiatric service animal. Psychiatric service animals are not emotional support animals. Their function is not to provide emotional support. Instead, they are trained to perform tasks detecting the onset of psychiatric episodes and lessen their effects (Younggren et al., 2016).

Alert dogs. Alert dogs are specially trained to alert their handlers and/or other caregivers to the onset of a medical condition or behavioral event. Their particular title is derived from the type of tasks they perform. Diabetic alert dogs warn a person when his or her blood sugar reaches high or low levels. Seizure alert dogs detect the onset of a seizure and assist the handler during and after the seizure. Dogs trained to assist children with autism may alert caregivers when repetitive behaviors occur or serve as a tether to prevent children from fleeing by going into a "down-stay" position if the child runs (Parenti et al., 2013). Each type of alert dog is considered a service dog under ADA if they are individually trained to perform behaviors needed by a person with a disability that they cannot do for themselves (Papalia, 2018).

Therapy animals. A therapy animal and its handler are certified as a team to provide comfort for people other than their handlers. Therapy animals provide stress relief, promote physical or emotional well-being, or assist during specific therapy sessions to help people meet specific goals. Therapy dogs are *not* service dogs and do not have public access rights. They may only enter buildings that allow pets with a direct invitation to the dog and handler or to the therapy dog organization (Papalia, 2018; Parenti et al., 2013).

Emotional support animals. Emotional support animals provide therapeutic comfort to an owner, who may or may not have a disability, through companionship, nonjudgmental positive regard, affection, and a focus in life. Emotional support animals are not service animals. They do not meet the ADA definition of a service animal because they are not individually trained to perform specific tasks for their handlers to mitigate a disability. In most cases, little specialized training is required. They do not have the same public access rights as service animals. However, they are afforded limited public access to housing as governed by the Fair Housing Act of 1988 and in airplanes by the US Department of Transportation (Schoenfeld-Tacher et al., 2017; Walther et al., 2017).

In review, the first step in ascertaining if an animal can enter a school is to determine if it meets the ADA definition for a service animal. Animals meeting the ADA definition must be provided access to the school. Those not meeting the definition are subject to the school or district pet policy and animal-related community regulations. Once the animal's ADA status has been affirmed, the second step in determining access is to establish the role of the handler.

Step 2: Determining the Role of the Handler

Before discussing specific handler roles, an important point about the handler, in general, must be made. The individual handling the service animal must be the person with a disability whom the animal is trained to support. Fundamentally, a service animal is afforded ADA protection when it is working for a person with a disability. Service animals accompanying an individual without a disability, such as a family member or friend, are not protected under ADA because they are not actively working. This is much the same as individuals who use a handicap parking placard. The individual with a disability is entitled to handicapped parking when using the vehicle, but that benefit is not technically afforded to family members when driving the car without the person with a disability present.

In addition to handlers with disabilities, some states and municipalities provide access to service animals in training if they are being actively trained or socialized. Some state or local laws cover animals in training to become service dogs when accompanied by their trainers. However, ADA does not apply. Laws regarding access to trainers vary because they provide additional protections beyond the scope of ADA (US Department of Justice, 2011).

The handler's role and the nature of the visit dictate the extent of school access afforded to service dogs. In general, school visitors, parents or guardians, and students are entitled to different levels of access. ADA guarantees equal access; thus an individual with a service animal is entitled to the same access as that provided to an individual with the same role. Details regarding each role are presented in the next section.

School visitors. Schools must permit service animals to accompany visitors with disabilities in all areas in which members of the public are allowed, including the cafeteria during a public fund-raising event, auditorium during a public exhibition, administrative offices, and gymnasium during a public sporting event. The ADA does not consider classrooms as public areas of the school. Exceptions include schools that do not receive federal funding or are controlled by a religious entity (Hildebrant, 2016).

Parents or guardians. A school must allow a service animal used by a parent/guardian of a student attending the school to accompany them in areas other parents/guardians are allowed. However, classroom access depends on specific school policies. If parents/guardians are permitted to visit the classroom, the service animal must be allowed to enter. However, if parents/guardians are not allowed to visit classrooms during the school day, a parent/guardian with a service animal can be denied access as well (Papalia, 2018).

Students. Student access is dependent upon the services the animal provides and the type of services the child receives. Students with a disability who do not receive special education or whose service dog is not included in their IEP can bring their service dogs anywhere pupils are permitted, including classrooms, hallways, and cafeterias. This right is afforded under the ADA and Section 504 of the Rehabilitation Act of 1973, legislation that provides equal access and prohibits discrimination based on disability. However, the service dog must perform activities directly related to the student's disability (Papalia, 2018).

Step 3: Determining Legal Protection Afforded

Students who receive special education and have a service animal included in their IEPs receive dual legal coverage. These students are provided equal access and protected from discrimination based on disability under the ADA and are protected under the Individuals with Disabilities Education Act (IDEA), which requires the school to provide a free appropriate public education to students with disabilities in the form of specialized instruction and related services.

Due process and dually covered students. When the school and family disagree over the need for the service dog, dual ADA and IDEA coverage can create controversaries and confusion because the family has two different avenues for seeking a legal remedy. Under IDEA, parents can appeal to the Department of Education if the school is not willing to allow the service animal in school and it is included in the student's IEP. Parents also can file a complaint with the US Department of Justice or file suit for discrimination in federal court under the ADA (Papalia, 2018). Determining which legislation applies under a given situation can be confusing; issues regarding free appropriate public education (FAPE) guaranteed under IDEA may also involve equal access protection guaranteed under ADA. The lines between these two laws are often blurred, leading to a second source of confusion regarding simultaneous litigation: must all remedies under one piece of legislation (e.g., IDEA) be exhausted before seeking due process under the other (e.g., ADA)? Dual coverage and the right to due process were the focus of a recent US Supreme Court case, *Fry v. Napoleon Community Schools*, involving the use of service dogs in schools (Papalia, 2018).

Fry v. Napoleon focused on Elhena Fry, a student with cerebral palsy who used a service dog named Wonder to assist her with everyday tasks. Her school provided her with a human aide in her IEP and refused to allow the service dog in school. The Frys sued the school, its principal, and the school district, alleging discrimination and denial of equal access and violations of ADA, Section 504, and state disability law. The district court found in favor of the school because the case involved Elhena's IEP, and the Frys were required to exhaust administrative remedies and request a due process hearing under IDEA before bringing a discrimination claim under ADA and Section 504. The Frys appealed, arguing the IDEA exhaustion provision does not apply because they were seeking relief from discrimination under ADA and Section 504 rather than objecting to the educational services. The US Court of Appeals for the Sixth Circuit found in favor of the school, indicating the case was essentially educational—although service dogs are not explicitly defined by IDEA, validity of the IEP is—therefore the IDEA's exhaustion requirement applied. The Frys appealed to the US Supreme Court, and the decision was reversed. The Supreme Court ruling indicated that exhaustion of the IDEA provisions was not necessary (*Fry v. Napoleon et al.*, 2017).

Within its decision, the US Supreme Court offered two hypothetical questions as a guide to distinguish between a violation of the free appropriate public education (FAPE) mandate of IDEA and discrimination as outlined in the ADA. First, could the same claim be brought if the issue occurred at a public facility that was *not* a school? And second, could an *adult* at the school have pressed essentially the same grievance? When the answer to those questions is yes, the denial of a FAPE is unlikely to be the focus of the case. But when the answer is no, then the complaint probably does concern a FAPE (even if the issue is not explicitly stated, as in the use of a service dog) because the FAPE requirement only applies to a child in the school setting (*Fry v. Napoleon et al.*, 2017).

Fry v. Napoleon Community Schools is a noteworthy case in that it directly addressed the issue of dual IDEA and ADA coverage for services dogs handled by students with disabilities who receive special education and provided some initial guidelines for addressing these issues. However, the case did not fully resolve the due process dilemma. As a result, further cases are likely to emerge addressing this same issue before clarifying the procedures (Papalia, 2018). Additional information about dually protected students is presented in chapter 7. One means of diminishing issues is to be proactive and for the individual with a service animal to use strategic handling skills.

STRATEGIC HANDLING SKILLS

Strategic handling skills are procedures designed to effectively introduce and sustain service animals used in a school setting. These skills are not legally mandated or meant to restrict the access of a service animal. Instead, they are devised to enhance understanding, support, and collaboration. Examples of these strategies include providing the school with advanced notice of a service arrival, educating students and school personnel on the legal protection afforded to service animals and service animal etiquette, and ongoing environmental assessments to support sustained use. Each of these strategies is discussed in the following section.

Prior Notice

Although not legally required, a student's family can notify the school in advance of the animal's arrival. This prior notice allows administrators to notify teachers and identify any potential issues such as a fear of animals or allergies. Fear of animals is not a valid reason for refusing a service dog to enter the school, but administration can alert these people to the potential location and travel patterns of a service animal to avoid contact. Schools can accommodate people with allergies by providing education in a separate space. For example, if a teacher or another student is allergic to dog dander, they can be placed in a different classroom than a person using a service animal or provide alternate locations for specific services (e.g., speech therapy or physical therapy) (US Department of Justice, 2011). Prior notice also allows teachers time to inform students of the service animal's presence and review service animal etiquette, such as not interfering with the service animal when it is working, not petting or feeding the service animal, and not drawing unnecessary attention to the person using the service animal. More specific information about service animal etiquette is included in chapter 9.

The service animal can visit class prior to attending full time to allow the students to meet the animal in a controlled situation. The visit also provides the animal exposure to its new environment and can identify any specific training needs to address. For instance, the service animal may react to the presence of other pets and may need some additional support or strategic placement within the class to avoid direct contact. (I was confronted with a similar situation when conducting a therapy dog visit to a classroom with a guinea pig named Caramel Peanuts. The therapy dog found a guinea pig, especially one with such a delicious name, quite intriguing; some additional training on the focus and leave-it commands as well as some initial distance from the cage were needed.)

Prior notice also allows for proactive planning for student support. Service animals are prone to the same illnesses and injuries as other animals. School personnel, family members, and the student may want to make arrangements for alternative services to those provided by the service animal in case the animal is injured, lost, or incapacitated for a time. For example, a classroom aide could help with balance or transfer issues for a student with a physical disability.

Legal and Service Dog Etiquette Information

School personnel should receive information regarding the legal access afforded to service animals in various parts of the school including the cafeteria, restrooms, and classrooms and when a service animal may be removed from a classroom. A school can ask a service animal to leave if it is not housebroken, barks excessively, or is out of control and the handler does not take effective action to control it. The student must be in control of the service dog. If not, an aide or trainer can accompany the student and the service dog. Responsibility for caring for the service dog should also be discussed. The student is also responsible for caring for the service dog including supervision, relief, and feeding when the dog is in school. If the student is too young or not capable of performing these duties, parents can work with the school to create an assistance plan until the student is comfortable handling the dog (Hildebrant, 2016).

Environmental Assessments

Environmental factors, such as classroom arrangement, travel patterns, and proximity to the handler, should be considered and assessed on an ongoing basis. For example, placement and storage of the service animals should be considered. Depending on the animal's function, close proximity to a handler may be required. Depending on the classroom arrangement, a service dog may need to lie under or beside a student's desk. Ample room is needed to accommodate a large dog or miniature horse. The arrangement and location of the desk should be considered to allow the dog space, to prevent the dog from blocking a highly traveled route within the classroom, and to minimize interference and injury to the animal. The service animal may also require a designated resting spot away from classroom activities to relax when it is not working, such as a soft rug or crate.

Environmental risk factors should also be examined. The service animal may require a designated resting place in a specific classroom, such as in a science lab to avoid contact with dangerous chemicals and noxious fumes. Potential contact between the service animal and other animals should be assessed. Some schools may allow therapy animals to visit classrooms or conduct therapy dog reading sessions in the library. Therapy animals should not be allowed to interact or interfere with the work of the service animal. Likewise, care should be taken to not allow pets visiting the school to interact with the service animal. School visits can be stressful situations for animals, and unintentional scuffles can occur. Injuries to a service animal or residual fears from an attack impact the animal's performance and the handler's quality of life. If a service animal is injured due to an accident at school, the school could be responsible. If a service animal is injured at school intentionally by another person, the person causing the injury could be liable for damages. If a service animal causes an injury, the handler, or the handler's family if they are a minor, could be accountable and their liability insurance applies.

SUMMARY

Determining the extent and nature of access for a service animal in school is a complex process. Access is determined based on a three-step framework: ADA status of the animal, nature of the visit, and legal coverage afforded for students based on services received. Several components of the ADA definition make identifying a service dog difficult. These components include a lack of identification and training requirements, restrictions on the type of allowable inquiries, and the use of the generic term *service animal* rather than a specific label indicating the animal's function. ADA guarantees equal access to people using service animals in schools. However, the extent of access differs depending on the role of the handler and the nature of the visit. The legal protection afforded to students using a service dog also depends on the services they receive. A student with a service animal who does not receive special education is protected under the ADA. A student who receives special education and has a service animal included in their IEPs receives dual legal coverage under IDEA and ADA. This dual coverage can make the resolution of due process complaints confusing because access and educational issues can overlap.

Strategic handling skills allow service animals to function effectively in the school environment. These skills involve planning in advance for the service animal's arrival and educating school personnel and students on legal information and service animal etiquette. Conduct periodic and ongoing environmental analysis of classroom arrangement and travel throughout the school to ensure safety and avoid interaction with people with allergies or fear of animals.

The scenarios presented at the beginning of the chapter involved access and strategic handling issues. This chapter concludes by applying the access framework and strategic handling skills to these situations with the hope that the solutions are more evident.

Moses and Orient

Moses is a fourth grader with a physical disability who uses a wheelchair. His parents are requesting that Moses's service animal accompany him while he is in school. His miniature horse named Orient performs tasks such as helping Moses balance while transferring to and from his chair and pulling the wheelchair up ramps when Moses is not able to climb them on his own. Mrs. Sellers, Moses's teacher, is concerned about Orient joining the class because one student in her class is allergic to horses and a speech therapist who visits the classroom is afraid of horses. Can Orient attend school with Moses? Why or why not?

- Yes, Orient can come to school with Moses.
- Orient meets the ADA definition of a service animal. Orient is individually trained to perform skills that Moses needs because of his disability (i.e., balance, transfer skills).
- Service animals cannot be excluded due to allergies or fear of animals. However, the student with allergies can be placed in a different classroom or placed as far from the service animal as possible within the classroom. The speech therapist can offer sessions in an alternate location.

Ming Lee and Elsie

Ming Lee is a tenth grader who experiences test anxiety. Her counselor recommended that Ming Lee bring her emotional support dog to school when Ming Lee takes tests. The dog, a Shih Tzu named Elsie, has lived with Ming Lee's family for the past three years. Ming Lee's parents noted that she tends to experience less anxiety when she holds Elsie in her lap. Can Elsie come to school on test days? Why or why not?

- Elsie does not meet the definition of a service animal and is not guaranteed access to the school; however, if the school's pet policy allows dogs in the classroom, Elsie can visit on test days.

Mr. Davidson and Radar

Mr. Davidson has two children enrolled in Mayfair Elementary School. He is coming to the school to drop off his daughter's lunch to the kindergarten classroom. Mr. Davidson has a specially trained psychiatric service dog that assists him due to PTSD. Mr. Davidson is in the school office and wants to bring his daughter's lunch directly to her classroom. The school secretary says that he must leave the lunch with her and cannot go to the classroom. Mr. Davidson becomes upset because he feels he is being denied access to the classroom because of his service dog, a rottweiler/Labrador retriever mix named Radar. Can Mr. Davidson bring his dog to the classroom? Why or why not?

- Yes, Mr. Davidson can bring his dog, Radar, into the school and receive the same level of access as other parents. However, he cannot bring Radar to the classroom because parents are not allowed in the classroom during instructional time.
- As an aside, service dogs cannot be denied access due to their breed.

Mrs. Rohena and Bright

Mrs. Rohena has diabetes and uses a diabetic alert dog named Bright. She is attending a high school musical, *Into the Woods*, to see her daughter perform. School personnel question her about bringing the dog and ask about the nature of her disability. Can Mrs. Rohena bring Bright to school? Why or why not?

- Yes, Mrs. Rohena can bring Bright to the play.
- Bright meets the definition of an ADA service animal because it is specially trained to perform a task mitigating Mrs. Rohena's disability that she cannot do for herself.

- Mrs. Rohena is a community member, and she and Bright are allowed the same access as other community members.
- Diabetes is an invisible disability. The school is not allowed to ask the nature of her disability; they may only ask if Bright is a service dog and the task the dog has been trained to perform.

Rosemary and Solomon

Rosemary volunteers at State Street Elementary School with her therapy dog, Solomon. The first graders read to the dog. Solomon is certified as a therapy dog by Therapy Dog International. A parent of a student in the class has complained to the first-grade teacher about the therapy dog visits because her son is allergic to dogs. Rosemary indicates to the teacher that Solomon can continue to visit the class regardless of allergies because he is a certified therapy dog and is entitled to rights under ADA. Can Solomon continue to visit the class? Why or why not?

- Solomon is not guaranteed access to State Street Elementary School because he does not meet the ADA definition of a service animal. Therapy dogs are specially trained to work with their handlers to provide support and comfort to others.
- Therapy dogs are invited to school settings, are subject to the school pet policy, and can be refused access due to allergies.

Jonas and Jinx

Jonas Scepter is a second-grade boy with autism who receives special education services. His IEP states he can bring his service dog, Jinx, to school. Jinx is a two-year-old golden retriever that recently completed service dog training. During the first few visits, Jinx was unruly in the classroom. He barked excessively, startling students and interrupting instruction. Jinx pulled away from Jonas on several occasions and ran from the classroom into the hall. Jinx also ate a part of another student's lunch while in the cafeteria. The principal asked Jonas's mother to keep Jinx at home. She refused, indicating the school is violating ADA by not allowing Jonas to bring Jinx in school because a provision for using a service dog is in Jonas's IEP. Can Jinx come to school? Why or why not?

- The principal can ask Jinx not to come to school until his training issues are resolved because Jonas cannot control the dog, Jinx is out of control. Jinx can receive further training, and an aide or trainer can accompany Jinx to school to help maintain control.

- Jonas receives protection under both IDEA and ADA because provision for using a service animal is included in his IEP. His parents can use the guidelines determined in the *Fry v. Napoleon* Supreme Court case to file for due process: could the same claim be brought if the issue occurs at a public facility that is *not* a school and could an *adult* at the school have pressed essentially the same grievance? If so, the denial of a FAPE is unlikely to be the issue and ADA applies. If not, it is likely a FAPE concern because it is occurring within a school setting and IDEA likely applies.

CHAPTER 7

SERVICE ANIMALS, STUDENTS WITH DISABILITIES, AND SPECIAL EDUCATION

It is wonderful when the service dog becomes a natural part of the environment. Some schools even include them in the student's yearbook photos.
—Kristin Hartness, Canines for Disabled Kids

> **ADVANCED ORGANIZER**
>
> Upon completing this chapter, you will be able to describe:
>
> - the dual protections of IDEA, ADA, and Section 504;
> - the differences in eligibility requirements for the three laws;
> - the differences in educational responsibilities for the three laws; and
> - dually protected students and service animals.

THIS CHAPTER PROVIDES an overview of the dually protected students (IDEA, ADA) who use service animals in the education environment. It also describes how it is legally decided who has permission to bring service animals to schools.

DUAL PROTECTION: IDEA VS. ADA AND 504

All students eligible for special education and related services in schools under the Individuals with Disabilities Education Act (IDEA) are also dually eligible under the Americans with Disabilities Act (ADA). This is also true for students who are also eligible under Section 504 of the Rehabilitation Act. Students eligible under IDEA receive all the protections of the other two laws. Chapter 3 describes each of these laws in detail. The following summary briefly highlights the differences between these laws by organizing them thematically.

Purpose
The different laws have distinct purposes. This section highlights the differences, whom they are for, and what to expect relating to their implementation.

IDEA. The IDEA is an education act that provides federal financial assistance to state and local education agencies to guarantee special education and related services to eligible children with disabilities.

ADA. The ADA is a civil rights law designed to prohibit discrimination solely on the basis of disability in employment, public services, and accommodations.

Section 504. Subtly different from ADA, Section 504 is a civil rights law designed to prohibit discrimination on the basis of disability in programs and activities, public and private, that receive federal financial assistance.

Eligibility

This section highlights the eligibility differences of the different laws. Not all individuals may be eligible under one law, but they may have eligibility under a different law. The differences between the laws may be minute, but it is important to understand which law to apply.

IDEA. There are some slight differences between who is eligible under the three laws. Under IDEA, all children ages birth to twenty-one are eligible if they are determined by a multidisciplinary team to first have a disability and second require the needs of a special education teacher. In order to be eligible, they have to have a disability in one of the following thirteen categories: autism, deafness, deaf-blindness, hearing impairments, intellectual disability, multiple disabilities, orthopedic impairments, other health impairments, serious emotional disturbance, specific learning disabilities, speech or language impairments, traumatic brain injury, and visual impairments.

ADA. ADA covers any individual with a disability who: (1) has a physical or mental impairment that substantially limits one or more life activities, (2) has a record of such impairment, or (3) is regarded as having such an impairment. Further, the person must be qualified for the program, service, or job.

Section 504. Section 504 covers any person who (1) has a physical or mental impairment that substantially limits one or more major life activities, (2) has a record of such an impairment, or (3) is regarded as having such an impairment. Major life activities include walking, seeing, hearing, speaking, breathing, learning, working, caring for oneself, and performing manual tasks.

Educational Responsibilities

This is where the three laws are different, especially as they relate to what schools need to provide for students with disabilities.

IDEA. Special education means "specially designed instruction at no cost to the parents, to meet the unique needs of the child with a disability." Related services are provided if students require them in order to benefit from education.

Students are to receive an appropriate education that is provided in accordance with their individualized education program at no cost to the parents.

ADA. There are no specific requirements for schools related to ADA. ADA protections do not apply to organizations, private schools, or entities controlled by religious organizations but do apply to nonsectarian private schools.

Section 504. Students eligible under Section 504 are to be provided an appropriate education, one that is comparable to their nondisabled peers. Section 504 does require development of a plan, although this written document is not mandated.

Evaluation

The evaluation of the student is often one of the most discussed parts of the program. The three laws take slightly different means of addressing this component.

IDEA. Prior to initiating services, all students are to receive a comprehensive multidisciplinary evaluation that highlights the needs the student has in relation to the general education curriculum. Once eligible, the process is to be reported every three years to ensure eligibility. Parental consent is required prior to the evaluation commencing. Students cannot start to receive special education services until after the evaluation is complete and the team, including the parents, discusses the results.

ADA. There are no specific guidelines related to evaluation measures for ADA.

Section 504. Though Section 504 does not require parental notice, a good practice is to obtain parental permission. The evaluation obtains data from a variety of sources and ensures the areas that need more concern are addressed. The evaluation needs to be documented, and all the evaluative data needs to be considered. Eligibility determinations are to be made by a team, not a single individual.

Placement

This section describes how the different laws treat the placement of students with disabilities in schools. Like the other sections described above, the differences may be subtle but are important for the reader to fully understand how the law applies.

IDEA. The placement decision is made based on the individual needs of the student, not on what is available. The placement is to be made so that the services provided are in the least restrictive environment as much as possible. The placement decision is then reflected in the student's IEP, and subsequent decisions about the services and location of those services need to be made by the IEP team.

ADA. Unlike the IDEA, the ADA does not specify evaluation and placement procedures. It does, however, specify provision of reasonable accommodations for eligible activities and settings. Reasonable accommodations may include but are not limited to: improved accessibility in the classroom, changing the presentation of tests and training materials, providing written communication in alternative formats, modifying tests, redesigning services to accessibility locations, altering existing facilities, and proving or adjusting a product, equipment, or software.

Section 504. Section 504 requires students to be educated with their nondisabled peers to the maximum extent appropriate. Section 504 does not require a meeting for any change in placement. The accommodations listed under ADA also apply.

SERVICE ANIMALS AND DUALLY PROTECTED STUDENTS

We have covered the differences between IDEA, ADA, and Section 504, and they are also highlighted in table 7.1. Section 504 is a civil rights law that prohibits discrimination against individuals with disabilities and, for a child with a disability, ensures equal access to an education. The child may receive accommodations and modifications. Under Section 504 of the Rehabilitation Act of 1973 (and the ADA), schools must permit the use of a service animal by a person with a disability. As noted in chapter 8, the IEP team does not have to provide the service animal and does not have to write the service animal into the student's program. It is the obligation of the school districts to provide a free appropriate public education (FAPE) regardless of whether the student chooses to bring a service animal to school (for more discussion of FAPE, see chapter 3).

The following are general guidelines related to an overall policy and discussions that staff administrators need to have with the staff. For more specifics, we have included a sample policy in the appendix.

- School staff may not ask about the person's disability.
- Staff may not require medical documentation, a special identification card, or training documentation for the dog.
- Staff may not ask the dog to demonstrate its ability to perform the work or task.
- When it is not obvious what task is being performed by a service animal, staff may ask only two questions:

    1. Is the dog a service animal required because of a disability?
    2. What work or task has the dog been trained to perform?

- Service animals are to accompany the individual with a disability in all areas of the school where students, visitors, and staff are normally allowed during school hours unless the service animal's presence or behavior creates a fundamental alteration in the nature of a facility's services in a particular area or is a direct threat to other persons in a particular area.

What is a direct threat?

Some animals may be perceived to be a threat to others. The following language is not meant as legal guidance but is intended to raise questions that should be addressed.

- A "direct threat" is defined as a significant risk to the health or safety of others that cannot be mitigated or eliminated by modifying policies, practices, or procedures.
- A person with a disability cannot be asked to remove their service animal from the premises unless the dog is not housebroken or is out of control or if the handler/owner does not take effective action to control the service animal.
- Fear and allergies are not valid reasons for denying access to a service animal or refusing service to people using service animals.
- People with disabilities who use service animals may not be isolated from others, treated less favorably than others, or charged with fees that are not charged to other customers without animals.
- Service animals must be harnessed, leashed, or tethered, unless these devices interfere with the service animal's work or if an individual's disability prevents using these devices. The handler/owner must then maintain control of the animal through voice, signal, or other effective controls.
- When encountering an individual with a disability, it is acceptable to ask if they need assistance. If yes, ask how you can best assist them.
- When encountering an individual with a service animal, do not interact with or distract the animal. (Public Health, 2020)

SUMMARY

Decisions regarding service animals should not be taken lightly. The individual with a disability may receive a clear benefit from the assistance provided. There are very important laws that provide guidance and clarification on the steps a school should take. We recommend users read the appendix at the end of this book, a sample policy for service animals in schools.

Table 7.1. Comparison of Laws Affecting Service Animals in Schools

	IDEA	ADA	Section 504
Purpose	Education law. Guarantees special education and related services to students up to age 21.	Civil rights law. Prohibits disability discrimination in employment, public services, and accommodations.	Civil rights law. Prohibits disability discrimination by public and private entities receiving federal funding.
Eligibility	0–36 Months (IDEA Part C); 3–21 years (IDEA Part B) with one or more of 13 identified categories. Determined by multidisciplinary team.	Not age restricted. Physical or mental impairment (or regarded as having such) that substantially limits one or more defined life activities. Individual must be otherwise qualified for service, program, or job. ADA does not apply to privately funded schools.	
Educational Responsibilities	Provided at no cost to parents. Specially designed, appropriate, individualized education program (IEP). Educationally beneficial related services. Defined in annual, written IEP.	None. Does not apply to privately funded schools.	Appropriate education comparable to nondisabled peers. Individual plan of accommodations and modifications.
Evaluation	Free, comprehensive, multidisciplinary evaluation conducted by school. Requires parental notification. Identifies specific educational needs of student. Reevaluated triennially.	Not specified.	Documented team evaluation. Parental notification not required (but we recommend it).
Placement	Based on needs of student, not current availabilities. Least restrictive environment. Made by IEP team (which includes parents). IEP team meeting required to approve any changes.	Not specified, except as related to reasonable accommodations.	With nondisabled peers to maximum extent possible. No meeting required for changes.

CHAPTER 8

IEPs AND SERVICE ANIMALS

The Individualized Education Program is the heart of the Education for All Handicapped Children Act as we wrote it and intended it to be carried out.
—Senator Robert Stafford, 1978, p. 72

ADVANCED ORGANIZER

Upon completing this chapter, you will be able to describe:

- the laws—and their differences—related to the education of students with disabilities,
- what an individualized education program or IEP is,
- the components of the IEP,
- the process for developing a legally defensible IEP, and
- the role of IEPs and service animals.

IN OTHER CHAPTERS, we have discussed the allowance in schools of service animals based on Section 504 and the Americans with Disabilities Act. This next section will discuss the Individuals with Disabilities Education Act (IDEA) and the obligations districts have to the provision of special education services as they relate to service animals in schools. This chapter will highlight the obligation of individualized education program (IEP) teams to ensure an appropriate education for the eligible student and will provide specific statements for IEP teams related to service animals. Districts need to offer a free appropriate public education (FAPE) to all eligible students prior to any discussion related to service animals. We discuss the development of appropriate IEPs and how to monitor FAPE and then follow with specifics for school districts to consider related to service animals.

LAW REVIEW

Before we discuss the roles of educators related to students eligible under IDEA and the role of IEP teams, we need to describe the differences between the various laws covering the education of students with disabilities in schools (for an in-depth discussion and comparison, see chapter 3). Specifically, we need to highlight that there are significant differences between Section 504 and IDEA. The most significant is that Section 504 is a civil rights law, whereas IDEA is an educational services law. For a child to be identified as eligible for services under Section 504, there are less procedural criteria governing the requirements of the school personnel. Section 504 is designed to provide necessary accommodations for individuals with disabilities. Its purpose is to ensure individuals with disabilities have the same access to education that individuals without disabilities have. This is done by eliminating barriers excluding individuals with disabilities from participating in school-related activities. Section 504 also covers the life span and safeguards the rights of persons with disabilities in many areas of their lives, including employment, public access to buildings, transportation, and education.

IDEA is narrower in scope than Section 504. Students eligible for services under the IDEA must meet specific criteria (see chapter 3). There is a higher degree of regulation with more specific time frames and parental participation requirements. In order for a student to be eligible under IDEA, they must first have a disability and also require the need for specially designed instruction like that provided by a special education teacher. IDEA also addresses the special education of students with disabilities from preschool to graduation only (from birth to age twenty-one). As an educational benefit or services law, IDEA offers additional services and protections for students with disabilities that are not offered to those without disabilities. All IDEA students are covered by Section 504, whereas not all Section 504 students are protected under IDEA.

The rights of the student eligible for special education are conveyed through an individualized education program or IEP. The IEP, which is provided only to students covered by IDEA, must be tailored to the child's unique needs and must result in progress for the eligible student. A Section 504 plan, on the other hand, provides accommodations based on the child's disability and resulting weaknesses but does not require academic improvement and does not have to be in writing.

An IEP is a written plan developed by a team that includes the school district personnel and the parents. It describes the program(s) and special services an eligible student requires to address their specific needs. The IEP is developed collaboratively by a multidisciplinary team including school staff and parents as well as related service staff if appropriate. All extra services that are to be provided to a student are to be listed in the IEP. Additionally, all services in the IEP are to be tied directly to the specific and individual educational needs of a student. IEPs may focus on social, academic, behavioral, and/or independence needs (i.e., daily living) depending on the area(s) of the student's need. It is a plan ensuring proper programming is in place to help the student eligible for special education to be successful at school. It is a working document that will be modified usually each year based on the ongoing needs of the student.

COMPONENTS OF THE IEP

This section addresses the components of the IEP as delineated in the federal regulations. The regulations related to IEP's can be found at 34 CFR Sec 300.320. The most important element of an IEP is the description of how the student is presently performing (Harmon et al., 2020). The present levels may be called various names depending on regional or state language such as present levels of performance (PLOPs), present levels of academic function (PLAFs), or other names indicating it describes the student's current performance. We will use the term present levels of academic achievement and functional performance (PLAAFP). Regardless of the nomenclature, this section is the foundation for the development of the IEP because it guides the team's decisions determining the types of instruction that should be delivered and the specific educational services that will be necessary to promote academic and functional growth.

The IEP team needs to ensure they include statements about student needs even if those needs are not tied directly to any specific curriculum. For all students, it is important IEP teams consider all areas of functional and academic performance. This is especially important if a service animal is being considered. For example, if a student has issues related to anxiety, there is not a specific academic need related to anxiety, but it is important for the team to develop a plan to address the student's needs. Another example would be a student who has issues related to diabetes; the school would need to highlight that and then develop a plan to address the needs.

For students who have primary needs that are academic and only receive special education and related services for academic needs, it is still very important to make note of present levels of functional performance (e.g., social, emotional, behavioral, communication, etc.). Parents and teachers are often asked to complete rating scales and checklists to provide formal evidence regarding typical functional performance. Anecdotal reports from teachers, parents, students, and other school staff members are also very important in developing a complete IEP.

WRITING LEGALLY DEFENSIBLE IEPs

To determine the necessary supports a student may need in school, the following steps need to occur. As was highlighted in the previous section, the program and services for the student are dictated by the needs presented in the present levels statements of the IEP. We are getting ahead of ourselves if we are discussing service animals for a student prior to discussing the student's needs. It is like putting the cart before the horse. The following steps help the IEP team in identifying the specific program for the student. We will address IEPs and service animals after this section.

The Process

The process of how a student goes from receiving general education without supports to receiving and making progress in special education is a very important one as highlighted in the recent *Endrew F.* Supreme Court decision (Yell & Bateman, 2020). In fact, the first part of the Supreme Court's definition of appropriateness has been referred to as: Part 1: Has the school district complied with the procedures of the IDEA?

First Step

The special education assessment is based on the reason for referral. Questions to ask include:
1. Is all the information complete and correct?
2. Does the report (and the IEP) clearly specify the student's disability?
3. As a part of the report, did the team identify how the student's disability affects their involvement and progress in the general education curriculum?

Second Step

The present level of academic achievement and functional performance is based on current assessment results and classroom performance. Make sure every need is described and that there is a goal or accommodation/modification for every need. Questions to ask include:
1. Is there information representing:
   - formal individually administered assessments?
   - general education teachers?
   - related services providers?
   - current statewide testing scores?
   - current levels of district and classroom benchmark tests?

- summary of student work samples?
- parental input?
- behavioral data?

Summary of the Report
1. Does the report clearly identify the student's needs and any strengths?
2. Are all of the concerns from the parent clearly identified?
3. Does the report contain current information (i.e., not just previous tests)?
4. Does the report clearly reflect the student's current performance in school?
5. Are all needs clearly identified in the summary?
6. Is the student making progress?

Third Step
The annual goals are directly related to the present level of academic achievement and functional performance. Questions to ask include:
1. Are the goals and objectives measurable?
2. Are all needs indicated in the present levels addressed?
3. Do the goals and objectives enable the student to make progress in the curriculum?
4. Do all of the goals and objectives tie directly to a need statement in the present levels?

Fourth Step
Any accommodations/modifications are based on and clearly related to the annual goals. Questions to ask include:
1. Was the determination of the appropriate aids and services and the special education and related services completed after the goals were finalized?
2. Are the services identified to support progress toward all goals including progress in the general education curriculum as well as other nonacademic activities?
3. Are all of the special education, related services, and any supplementary aids based on peer-reviewed research to the extent practicable?
4. Are the start times clearly delineated for all services?

Fifth Step
The placement for the student is made after the annual goals are developed. Questions to ask include:
1. Are all decisions for services based on providing education in the least restrictive environment?

2. Are all decisions for placement of services made *after* the goals and objectives have been completed?
3. Do the services provided allow the student to be educated with typically developing peers and access to the general education curriculum, to the maximum extent possible?
4. Is there a clear description of the location of the services to be provided, and if necessary, why the services cannot be provided in the child's home school?
5. Is there a clear description of the amount of time the student will be participating in the general education classroom?
6. Does the educational setting clearly support the goals for the student?

Sixth Step (if needed)
A behavioral intervention plan is developed if there is an indicated need. Questions to ask include:
1. Is the targeted behavior clearly described in observable terms?
2. If there is a replacement behavior, does it serve the same need for the student as the problem behavior?
3. Are member(s) of the IEP team clearly identified who will be responsible for taking data related to the behavior intervention plan? How will the data be communicated to the team?
4. What services will the student need to successfully implement the behavior intervention plan and meet their goal?

Seventh Step (if needed)
A transition plan is developed if the student is sixteen years old (younger in some states). Questions to ask include:
1. Is there an appropriate measurable postsecondary goal or goals that cover education or training, employment, and, as needed, independent living?
2. Are the postsecondary goals updated annually?
3. Are the postsecondary goals based on age-appropriate transition assessments?
4. Are there transition services in the IEP that will reasonably enable the student to meet his or her postsecondary goals?
5. Does the course of study reasonably enable the student to meet their postsecondary goals?
6. Is there an annual IEP goal related to the student's transition service needs?
7. Was the student invited to and involved in their transition planning?
8. Was a representative of any participating agency invited to the IEP team meeting with prior consent from parent, guardian, or student?

Progress

The IEP must be developed using this process and also must be reasonably calculated to be able to measure the student's progress. To facilitate planning and preparation for the year, it is often helpful to think about this as three distinct phases.

- first, a calculation about what the student may be expected to achieve during the year;
- second, regular monitoring of the student's progress throughout the year; and
- third, an analysis of progress toward the goals at the annual IEP meeting.

Expected progress. The Supreme Court was clear in the *Endrew* decision that the IEP must be calculated to enable a student eligible for special education and related services to make progress appropriate in light of his or her circumstances (Yell & Bateman, 2020). This can be done by considering two factors:

1. Review the present levels of academic achievement and functional performance. It is important to clearly delineate every possible need that a student has. Some suggest we pay attention to the disability, but one must remember that each disability is an umbrella term that often only serves as a gatekeeping function to ensure students are eligible for services.
2. Examine the potential for growth. Where can the student be reasonably expected to be functioning after a year's worth of intensive services?

When considering these two factors, it is very important for the goals to be ambitious (Yell & Bateman, 2020). This is done to ensure that all the assessment data informs the present levels. The PLAAFP statements really are the basis for the foundation of the student's educational program. They inform the goals, both academic and behavior, and any accommodations along with modifications. After this, the goals and the levels of support needed provide guidance in the placement decisions.

Annual progress. The shift in focus should be on if the student has made educational progress. This is measured by the student's progress toward their goals. The goals are expected to be ambitious. However, does the student have to master all of his or her goals in order to have made progress? The courts are not clear on how much is enough, nor are they clear on whether five out of six is enough or if one out of seven is good. It is important that, if a student is not making progress on their goals, the same things did not occur throughout the year without change. Make a change.

Each and every goal should be analyzed not only annually but at the end of each marking period to determine if progress is being made. Based on the progress, or lack thereof, the IEP team should use any additional information that is covered on the PLAAFP statement to develop or modify the goals for the student, in addition to the data from the previous marking period. One of the big problems in the *Endrew* case was that goals were repeated from year to year (Yell & Bateman, 2020). The repetition of goals each year could likely indicate a lack of progress from the previous year. If the team does find a goal(s) where the student is not making progress, it is imperative for the team to adjust the goal and potentially assess to determine whether the student has the necessary pre-skills to complete the task and to determine if there are other issues preventing goal mastery.

Suggested IEP Practices

The following should help IEP teams in the development and implementation of IEPs. Not every suggestion will apply as the IEP is an individualized program for the eligible student.

- Ensure that the IEP team has all the evaluation information needed to make the required IEP decisions.
- Routinely send evaluation reports to parent(s) and IEP team members before the meeting is convened.
- Set a meeting agenda for each IEP team meeting.
- Provide a reference set of IEP forms for each team member.
- Eliminate educational jargon within IEPs.

As the school district develops the technology to do so, we recommend at the end of a team meeting that the parent be provided with a copy of the developed IEP. If a full, neat copy is unavailable at the end of the meeting, we recommend that parents receive the sections related to goals and objectives and services, even if such information is provided in rough draft form.

IEP Development Is a Student-Driven Process

Once a student has been found eligible for special education services, an IEP must be developed. The IEP must address the unique needs of the student and, therefore, must be tailored to the individual student needs as determined through the evaluation process. Good IEPs will be responsive to parent concerns and the student's vision and will assist the student as much as possible to move toward independence.

The IEP is intended to be a useful document that helps educators and parents to understand the student and how best to work with that student. In other words, the IEP should describe how the student learns, how the student best demonstrates learning, and how the school staff and the student will work together to help the student learn better. The IEP is not intended to be a daily, weekly, or monthly lesson plan but should provide a clear picture of the student's current abilities and needs and should identify key goals and objectives that provide a direction and focus for the student's learning over the next IEP period. If carefully and thoughtfully written, the IEP will serve as a vehicle for improving the educational experience and results for a student with disabilities.

Although IEP development is a student-driven, individualized process, there are some central concepts that should be adhered to during a well-managed team meeting. A well-managed team meeting will:

- obtain parent/student input,
- think about the student's future dreams and goals,
- understand how the student's disability(ies) affects the student's learning,
- know how the student performs today,
- address only the areas that are affected by the disability(ies),
- provide a focus for the student's learning during the designated IEP period,
- reflect high expectations for the student,
- stay as close as appropriate to what the student's peers are learning and doing, and
- identify supports and services the student needs for success.

Placement

The IEP forms the basis for the placement decision. Therefore, the IEP must be developed in its entirety before placement is decided. The placement and services decision must be based on a careful reflection of the IEP, including the services that the team has identified as necessary and the impact of the disability on the student's learning. Finally, the team must be mindful of the requirements related to placement in the least restrictive environment. Teams need to remember that removal from the classroom solely because of needed program modifications is not permissible. Only after the needs of the student and the types of services have been discussed by the team and agreed to in an IEP can the placement be effectively chosen by the team.

The IEP is written to fit the student. The placement is chosen to fit the IEP.

The IEP under no circumstances should be written "to fit" a particular placement. Teams must remember this critical fact when moving through the team process to ensure that the IEP is written to address the unique needs of the student.

Teams Must Do the Right Thing

Laws and regulations tightly control the IEP process. IEPs should be developed to ensure not only that teams are in compliance with the myriad rules and regulations related to the IEP but that students make progress. However, the best reason to carefully follow the process and its key elements, as listed below, is to ensure positive student-centered results:

Key Elements of the IEP Process
- Assess in all areas related to the suspected disability(ies).
- Consider access to the general curriculum.
- Consider how the disability affects the student's learning.
- Develop goals and objectives that make the biggest difference for the student.
- Ultimately choose a placement in the least restrictive environment.

SERVICE ANIMALS

We have spent the majority of this chapter discussing school districts' role in providing a FAPE to eligible students. This is an obligation of districts regardless of whether a service animal is discussed. We also need to highlight that when there is a discussion of the student's programming, there may be phrases related to "the best education" or the need to "maximize the education" of the student. Just to clarify as we move into the service animal section of this chapter, there is no obligation of school districts to provide the best or optimal education for the student or to maximize the student's educational outcomes. The only obligation is that students receive an appropriate education. This has been affirmed in the only two Supreme Court cases that have been heard on this issue (*Endrew F.*, 2017; *Rowley*, 1982).

Specifically, what should districts do related to service animals? First, as noted repeatedly throughout this chapter, the district must provide a FAPE to the student. It is not a requirement to provide the student a service animal nor is the school required to train a service animal. Don't write the service animal in the student's plan unless it's required by FAPE.

If the parents believe a service animal is necessary, then the district should note in the IEP or the Section 504 plan that the student has a service animal provided by the parents to meet certain needs. Importantly, however, the district needs to clarify how the school district is addressing the student's needs to ensure the student receives FAPE (see above section of this chapter). The district absolutely has an obligation to provide FAPE. This obligation is necessary for the student regardless of the discussion of a service animal.

Is a service animal necessary for the student to receive FAPE? FAPE is defined at 34 CFR 10433(b) as the provision of an appropriate education and the provision of regular or special education and related aids and services that are designed to meet individual educational needs of handicapped persons as adequately as the needs of nonhandicapped persons are met. As noted above, go through all of the student's needs and identify how they will be addressed. For every need, the IEP team should strategically consider how the IEP will address said need.

If it is determined a student does not need a service animal because the district can address the needs of the student otherwise, it needs to be made clear in the IEP or Section 504 plan. A sample statement might be: "We don't think the student needs a dog to achieve FAPE, but we recognize that your child has a right to have a dog here in accordance with Section 504." Make sure the team and especially the parents (as members of the team) know the district is meeting the student's needs and the district is allowing the student to have a dog as long as the dog meets the criteria of a service animal (see chapter 4).

For purposes of education, it is important to note emotional support animals do not qualify as service animals under the Title II regulations. The US Department of Justice, however, has stated such animals may be permitted reasonable accommodations under other laws, suggesting that an emotional support animal might qualify as a reasonable accommodation if necessary for the student to receive FAPE, even though it would not meet the definition of a service animal under Title II. Districts, as noted above, need to address the needs of the student and ensure they have appropriate supports available. Additionally, the distinction between a psychiatric service animal and an emotional support animal turns on the work or tasks the animal performs. While emotional support animals provide comfort or companionship, psychiatric service animals perform tasks such as reminding an individual with a disability to take medication, performing safety checks or room searches for individuals with PTSD, interrupting self-mutilation, and removing disoriented individuals from dangerous situations (*Federal Register*, volume 75, p. 56195 [September 15, 2010]).

Even though a district has determined it is providing a FAPE to the eligible student, they should not exclude a service animal outright without considering the specifics of the student's situation and his individualized needs. The outright exclusion of a service animal may be a Title II or Section 504 violation, as the IDEA is silent on these accommodations for eligible students. Although a number of hearings have found districts do not have to permit the use of a service dog absent a showing of educational need, those decisions focus solely on the obligations of FAPE under the IDEA.

IEPs and Service Animals

Make sure the district is providing a free appropriate education to the student. The IEP must be developed based on the student's needs and also must be reasonably calculated to measure student progress. To facilitate planning and preparation for the year, it is often helpful to think about this as three distinct phases.

- first, a calculation about what the student may be expected to achieve during the year;
- second, regular monitoring of the student's progress throughout the year; and
- third, an analysis of progress toward the goals at the annual IEP meeting.

Tips for School Districts under IDEA for Service Animals

The following are tips for school districts about the implementation of the IDEA requirement that a student receives a FAPE and service animals. Some of the suggestions will clearly repeat other sections of this book as they relate to requirements under Section 504 and the ADA. The following is not legal advice, and for specific instances, school districts are encouraged to review their specific state laws relating to service animals and to consult their individual attorney for guidance and recommendations. The following, however, are based on recommendations provided by legal counsels across the nation and will serve as guidance that will assist in developing specific questions for your legal counsel.

- School districts may ask whether the service animal is required because of a disability and ask about the work or task the animal is to perform.

It is recommended for school districts to not ask these questions when it is apparent the animal is trained to do work or perform tasks for an individual with a disability.

- Complete an inquiry about whether the service animal is an appropriately trained service animal.
- Complete an inquiry to determine if the service animal performs a specific disability-related task for the student.
- Ensure (as noted above) that all of the needs of the student are covered by the district in the IEP through the necessary services.
- Meet as an IEP team to determine if the service animal is necessary for the student to receive FAPE.
- Barring evidence, do not assume a service animal poses a health risk to the staff and students.
- Barring evidence, do not assume a service animal poses a safety risk to the staff and students.
- If, after the IEP determines the district can provide FAPE, the parents want the student to have a service animal, reconvene the team and ensure the IEP reflects the district has an offer of FAPE and the parents will be providing a service animal for the student.
- Districts may not prohibit the use of service animals on school grounds or lead parents, students, or the community to believe that service animals are not welcome at schools.
- Generally, districts are not responsible for the "care and supervision" of service animals, such as by providing a tether or a trained handler. However, in some cases, the district may need to assist a student with the care of their service animal in order to satisfy the ADA's reasonable accommodations requirement.
- A school district may not require the family to pay a surcharge, even if it requires individuals with pets to pay a fee or to comply with other requirements that do not apply to people without pets. However, a school district may charge a family for any damage caused by a service animal.
- A school district may not require documentation from the family (or the student) regarding proof the animal has been certified, trained, or licensed as a service animal.
- A number of due process hearings have found a district does not have to permit the use of a service dog absent a showing of educational need. Districts need to not just determine if a service animal is necessary for FAPE but also consider the district's duty under the ADA to provide students with disabilities "equal access" to its facilities.

- In the *Fry* case, the Supreme Court stated students whose service animals have been excluded from school may file disability discrimination claims under Title II of the ADA even if they have received FAPE under the IDEA (*Fry v. Napoleon*, 2017). Make sure the district is providing FAPE and is not discriminating.
- State codes may provide guidance that districts must permit service animals to accompany students with disabilities at all school functions, whether inside or outside of the classroom. Read your specific state code related to service animals.
- Be careful about excusing a service animal if there is a determination that a different student may be allergic. There have been multiple cases finding the presence of students with allergies in a school did not excuse a district's decision to ban a service animal from the building.
- The nondiscrimination aspects of service animals apply to parents and others participating in school-related events. Districts must afford parents and others with disabilities the same opportunities to participate in district programs and activities that nondisabled parents have. This means that a district can't require parents with service animals to meet additional participation requirements.
- The Office of Civil Rights has made multiple determinations indicating districts should not exclude a service animal from school grounds before conducting a direct threat assessment.
- If a district has reason to believe that the presence of a service animal poses a health or safety risk to others (including students and staff), the district should evaluate to determine what precautions it needs to take.
- The IDEA (and also the ADA) clearly does not address the rights of students who are nondisabled who are training dogs to be service animals, but many state laws grant service animals in training equal rights as service animals. Check state law for guidance on whether nondisabled students have the right to bring service animals in training on school grounds.

Finally, there is an expectation that students eligible for special education under the IDEA need to exhaust their administrative remedies before going to either state or federal court with a complaint about the services they are receiving. This means that a student needs to have a due process hearing on the issues relating to FAPE. Students who have filed cases in state or federal court have been told they need an administrative hearing on issues related to FAPE. This might not be the case when a service animal is involved. But if there is a question of whether the student received FAPE, an administrative hearing is absolutely necessary.

When might a student with a service animal not need to go through the IDEA administrative procedures? A recent Supreme Court case (*Fry v. Napoleon*) held parents of a five-year-old girl with cerebral palsy may not need to go to a special education due process hearing before pursuing Section 504 and ADA claims against a Michigan district that had excluded their child's service dog from school. In a rare unanimous decision, the Supreme Court clarified the IDEA's exhaustion requirement only applies when the gravamen of the complaint is a denial of FAPE. The Court noted in determining whether a complaint seeks relief for a denial of FAPE, lower courts should consider two hypothetical questions: First, could the student assert the same claim against a public entity other than a school, such as a library? Second, could an adult at the school assert the same claim against the district?

If the answer to those questions is yes, the claim is unlikely to involve a denial of FAPE. The Supreme Court noted the parents in this case never disputed the appropriateness of their child's IEP or her receipt of FAPE. The parents alleged in their complaint the service dog's exclusion denied their child equal access to the district's facilities. The Court pointed out the parents could have filed essentially the same discrimination claims if any other public space had refused admittance to the child's service animal. Likewise, an adult visitor with a service animal when visiting the school could have sued the district for preventing him from entering.

SUMMARY

Districts are responsible for providing FAPE to students eligible for special education and related services. FAPE is built upon developing an appropriate program that is individualized to the student and addresses their needs in the least restrictive environment. The IDEA and Section 504 and Title II have different rules and requirements related to obligations of service. Pay attention to the IEP and ensure the student receives a FAPE. The rules for schools related to service animals fall under Section 504 and Title II.

CHAPTER 9

SERVICE ANIMALS IN SCHOOL

Implications for Administrators, Teachers, and Parents

Knowing the various types of animals as they are legally defined, educational leaders have a better understanding of creating environments supportive of service animals. Logistical, practical, and procedural contexts require examination when developing policy that can be well communicated to all stakeholders.
—Kathy B. Ewoldt et al., "Service Animals in PreK–12 Schools"

ADVANCED ORGANIZER

By the end of this chapter, you will be able to:

- understand administrative considerations for service animals in schools,
- understand parental concerns for service animals in schools,
- identify logistics required when service animals are in schools, and
- know behavioral expectations of adults and children around service animals in schools.

SERVICE ANIMALS IN SCHOOLS are projected to become increasingly prevalent, and therefore school leaders are wise to explore the logistics of welcoming service animals onto their campus. To do so in a manner that balances the sometimes competing needs of all individuals who come to school requires a consideration of multiple perspectives and a willingness to welcome all. This chapter discusses points administrators and parents should consider when a service animal will be part of the classroom experience.

POLICIES

Earlier chapters in this book address the legal codes and regulations defining service animals and the requirements defined by legislation, regulations, and previous case laws that provide guidance on how to best address service animals in education (for example, see chapters 3 and 4). The consideration of district and/or building policy will further guide those who interact with service animals on your campus. Local institutes of higher education may have established policies, which would likely take into account local and state requirements; these policies can serve as a framework for developing PK–12 policies (Ewoldt, Dieterich, & Brady, 2020). Additionally, this book's appendixes contain a sample policy and a policy development framework to help guide leaders as they create their own policies for animals on campus.

PLANNING FOR A SERVICE ANIMAL

There are many things to consider prior to the arrival of a service animal on campus. Logistical considerations for the animal and the people who will have direct and indirect contact with the animal should be included in the planning process.

Verification of the necessity of the service animal by the handler is guided by the definition of a service animal and the associated questions allowed. There are only two questions that may legally be asked of an individual with an animal:

1. Is your animal a disability-related service animal?
2. What task has your animal been trained to perform?

These questions establish the legitimacy of the animal (for further discussion, see chapter 4). Once the animal is deemed a service animal, the real planning can begin.

Animal

Although there are no legal requirements for service animal certification or registration, schools should consider a central location for the administration and oversight of animal-related services such as the dean's office or the school nurse. For this conversation, we will use the term *administration office*. The purpose of the administration office is to have a single, central location for oversight and communication. This office should contain any written policies related to service animals, tracking mechanisms for animals on campus, records related to service animals, and mitigation procedures when discrepancies arise. Recommended considerations can be found in table 9.1.

Table 9.1. Central Administration Considerations

Oversight	Name of office that will oversee service animal administration/coordination on the school/district site.
Student Information	Name, ID number, class schedule with room numbers and times.
Service Animal Information	Name, handler's contact info, parent's contact info, IEP/Section 504 case manager contact info, immunization record (if applicable).
Local Requirements	State service animal laws/regulations, county/city animal requirements.
Cross-check	Examine intersection of room locations/times in which any students with allergies may be in the same locations service animal is/has been.
Training	Specific staff who will encounter service animal (e.g., cafeteria, maintenance, teachers, itinerant faculty, counselors).
Review	Frequency of service animal reviews (e.g., once/academic year, every fall), date this specific service animal will be due for review (e.g., when immunizations expire).

Note: We recommend a specific school/central administration person be assigned to each task to clarify roles and responsibilities.

Administration offices may ask for immunization records of service animals on campus to ensure the safety of everyone. However, as stated previously, a lack of providing school-requested documents cannot be a reason to exclude service animals from campus (see chapter 7). Administrative offices should consider keeping a master schedule of the locations that will have service animals and during which times of the school day. This master schedule can be used to mitigate potential conflicts. For example, if there are students on campus who have allergies, this master schedule would be useful to ensure the animals and the student(s) are never in the same space at the same time and/or there is ample cleaning between the animal and the individual using a single space. Additionally, if there are individuals on campus with zoophobia, which is fear of animals, having a master schedule can aid in ensuring everyone is accommodated to the greatest extent possible.

Administrators should consider full communication with all school users when a service animal will be part of the community. Staff, students, parents, and visitors should be made aware of the existence of a service animal. Issues can be avoided when everyone is informed of the animal's presence. In addition to an initial notification of an animal on campus, administrators could consider including information on the presence of a service animal on campus in the regular communication tools such as newsletters and websites. Should people be resistant to the presence of the animal, education may be enough to overcome the issue. Administrators will need to be aware of speaking in generalities so that an individual's health and/or educational information is protected (e.g., HIPAA, FERPA) and in accordance with local identity protection regulations. Being well-informed of the purpose and necessity of service animals may allay reservations regarding or resistance to service animals on campus. Additionally, mitigation may be necessary. This may be as simple as a scheduling change or a relocation of events.

Relief. Administrators will need to consider a designated area for animals to relieve themselves. These areas should be considerate of accessibility for the animal handlers, the safety of the animal and students, and the aesthetics of the environment. These areas should be regularly cleaned to prevent unsanitary conditions, which will also require considerations of which maintenance and/or custodial staff will be responsible and how often and which types of cleaning products will be used. Commercial products may need to be purchased to remove solid waste (e.g., rakes, shovels, bags) as well as odors (e.g., enzyme-based liquids). The frequency of waste removal may depend on local environmental factors. For example, areas of high humidity and rainfall would require more immediate attention whereas in arid climates a daily removal may suffice. Relief area designation and expectations should be clearly delineated and communicated to all stakeholders.

Transitions. The service animal's movement about the campus will be dependent upon the necessary movement of the handler. Secondary students will likely have more frequent transitions than elementary students. During times of passing from one location to another, administrators should consider the expected behaviors of the handler, the animal, and the other passers-by. The handler must be in control of the animal at all times, including times of passing. However, this control may not necessarily include a leash (see chapter 3), which could cause concern for passers-by with fears of animals. Depending on the nature of the transitions, administrators could consider an accommodation for an alternate passing time for the handler and service animal. However, this should be as a last resort so that the student can have maximum inclusion with peers.

People

Educating everyone who has access to the campus and who may come in contact with the service animal is critical to the successful integration of service animals into the school community. All students and staff should be educated on the proper interaction with animals who are working (see Dos and Don'ts below). It's important for everyone to understand that service animals are not classroom pets and are not providing any support or therapy to others. They are there solely to work for their person. Roles of certain people on campus will dictate the type of information and training required. Similar to the custodial staff being informed of relief issues as described above, cafeteria staff should also be notified of a service animal's presence and be included in the conversation of establishing protocols and expectations for behavior. For example, is there adequate space for the individual to navigate all public areas of the cafeteria? The same list of dos and don'ts listed below for children should also be communicated to staff and faculty.

Training

As policies are being developed, administrators should consider a wide audience of individuals who should be included in the conversations such as teachers, custodians, parents, and students. After development, staff and faculty will need to be educated on the adopted policies and procedures. Administrators could consider the frequency and depth of training depending upon the individual roles of staff and faculty. For example, some staff will have little interaction and may not need as thorough training as someone who will have day-to-day interaction with the service animal. Tracking the completion of this training could also be considered and overseen by the designated administrative office. Of particular importance are the two allowed questions that can be asked of individuals with service animals (see chapter 7). All students should also be trained on behavior expectations when they encounter a service animal.

Children. It is important to prepare and train children before they will interact with a service animal. Children should understand that service animals are working hard to keep their person safe and any distractions could jeopardize safety. Sometimes, working animals may not be easily recognized so it is important to always ask the owner before petting or approaching someone's animal. Service animals are allowed to go in places other animals and pets are not allowed, which may be a surprise to students. Children should also know that although many service animals can be recognized by a special vest, collar, or leash, sometimes even animals that are not labeled might be working.

Ignoring the service dog and allowing them to keep their person safe is recommended, but students' curiosity and questions should be answered, particularly for younger children. Students could be taught several different services that dogs may provide in general but should also be discouraged from asking an individual about the specifics of their disability and the tasks their dog performs.

Students should understand that certain behaviors should not occur around a service dog because they could potentially cause harm. For example, service dogs should never be fed or offered drinks. Students should not shout, make loud noises, or whistle. Anything that distracts the dog from their job should be avoided.

Do:
- ask before petting any animal,
- look at the dog's tail (e.g., wagging means I'm happy; tail between my legs means that I am worried),
- pet gently along the back toward the tail,
- give the dog and person the right of way, and
- try to ignore the dog as much as possible so she or he can work.

Don't:
- shout, whistle, or make loud noises;
- get too close too quickly;
- touch without asking;
- offer food or drinks to the dog;
- be surprised if you are not allowed to pet the dog; or
- ask specifics about the person's disability.

Mitigation

In addition to fears and allergies addressed above, administrators should consider policy and procedures for cleanliness, zoonosis, and uncontrolled service animals. Administrators should also consider how to respond to complaints and less specific resistance by stakeholders. Schools can require animals to be clean and pest free. If the animal is ill, it should not attend school until the issue is addressed.

Lack of control and/or lack of the animal being housebroken are reasons a service animal can be excluded from the campus. For example, if the service dog is running around and chasing other students, and the individual with a disability cannot control the dog, this behavior is a reason to consider either not allowing the animal on campus or seeking additional training for both the dog and the individual.

To mitigate other forms of resistance by stakeholders who may not have experience, administrators who are well-educated on the local and national laws and protections afforded to service animals should be equipped to handle a variety of issues that could arise. Remember, the legal requirement is access to the goods and services of the institution, with the service animal being there to assist the person with a disability to be able to participate and not to be discriminated against based on their disability.

WHAT PARENTS SHOULD KNOW

Service animals in schools are provided protection under the Americans with Disabilities Act. Students with service dogs may also be protected under the Individuals with Disabilities Education Act (see chapter 7 for discussion). Your child may already have a service animal and be transitioning to a new school. Or perhaps your child having a service animal is a new situation for your family. Regardless, open and frequent communication with the school will provide an experience conducive to a supportive learning environment for all.

Parental involvement in education promotes positive academic outcomes and may explain why IDEA mandates that schools collaborate with parents. The power and importance of the parent's role in their child's education cannot be overstated. Parents have been their child's earliest and longest-tenured educator and bring an unmatched level of understanding to their child in a multitude of different situations and levels of success (Reid & Weatherly Valle, 2004). The parent's unique perspective adds a significant understanding when considering the whole child. Parents should be a part of all meetings regarding services, along with regular contact to ensure the process is working from their perspective.

Notification

Notifying the school as early in the transition process as possible will allow time to plan for the animal on campus. While you as the parent are most concerned about your child, the administration has a wider audience to consider including your child, the other students, custodians, clerks, bus drivers, cafeteria and other staff, faculty, and community members who come to campus. Administrators with prior experience with service dogs have already been educated on the protections provided to service dogs. However, those with less experience may require more education. The parent can provide valuable and necessary information to the school leaders. Successful parent and school partnerships have been shown to increase positive academic outcomes for students (Powell et al., 2010).

Advocacy

The service animal will attend the school with the same purpose(s) as times she or he accompanies the individual with a disability to any other location. Dealing with the interest and behaviors of the public may have been part of the training received when the service animal was acquired. Parents may have already learned how to respond to a variety of situations, depending on the length of time their child has used the services of a service animal. However, the school setting may bring additional considerations because of the nature of having many young people in one location. The situations that arise could also vary depending on the education and experience of the administration, faculty, and staff at the school.

The administration may need to be educated on the rights afforded to service animals (and service animals in training) in a local community, the questions that can and cannot be asked, and their responsibilities to accommodate service animals (see chapters 3, 4, and 7). In the classroom, the teacher and the students may need to be educated on proper interactions and behaviors with and of a service animal. This may include the need to help others understand that the service animal attends school for the benefit of the individual with a disability only. Although there may be positive benefits to having a service animal in the classroom, those are purely ancillary. A service animal is not a classroom pet nor there to provide any other services to anyone except the specific child. Parents may need to advocate for this understanding.

Logistics

When discussing school attendance of the individual with a disability and their service animal, a few matters of logistics around relief, cleanliness, paperwork, and behavioral expectations should be discussed with the administrator and perhaps the classroom teacher. They should then be responsible for disseminating the information to other staff such as the cafeteria personnel and the custodial staff.

One of the major concerns with animals on school grounds is relief. Many service animals are trained to relieve on command and may only need one or two relief breaks during the day. When these occur, the child should know exactly where the relief area has been designated and the expectations for cleaning solid waste. This is a critical discussion to have with administrators, to include who will remove the waste, how often it will be removed, and where it will be disposed. The child may need to clean it immediately, or another designated adult may be needed to assist with transition from the classroom to the relief area. Perhaps this adult will remove the solid waste? Or in other cases the custodial staff may be required. As much as possible, the individual with a disability should remove the waste and dispose of it properly. This is the best arrangement for building goodwill with the school campus but is not always possible depending on the needs of the student—which should always come first.

Logistical conversations with the administration and teacher should also include daily navigation around the classroom and the school. A typical day at school will include physical movement in and around a variety of locations. For example, there should be discussions regarding the entry to the campus itself, entry to the classroom, transitions to the cafeteria, and transitions to "specials" such as music, art, and physical education. Discussions should include who will be moving about at which times, where they will go and not go, and the behavioral expectations during these times of relocation. Parents may consider requesting access to all of the locations the animal will attend prior to the service animal's first day at school. Allowing the animal to navigate the entire campus and perhaps interacting with the associated staff during this "dry run" will allow all parties involved to see how these movements will occur. Having the individual with a disability and their service animal do this practice may reveal some interesting situations such as possible physical barriers or classrooms that are too cluttered with furniture or other items.

Although most days will be typical, there are also other predictable routines that should be discussed such as fire drills or special assemblies. Have a discussion about emergency procedures and other unplanned circumstances that could arise. The logistics of navigating these locations and situations should also be clearly communicated prior to their need so that everyone is fully aware of the expectations.

Service animals should attend school properly cleaned, groomed, and free of pests. Regular cleaning and grooming promotes health and happiness for your service animal and removes a potential source of conflict with the school. If your service animal becomes infested with pests, the animal should not attend school until the infestation has been fully mitigated.

Finally, only service animals specifically trained to work in crowded situations should be used to provide supports for the individual with a disability as they attend school. Many people are unfamiliar with the roles of service animals or the differences between service animals and emotional support animals, and we need to ensure that the staff are receiving the correct information about what is expected, but also the family and the individual with a disability need to remember they are the model for others and to represent others with service animals appropriately.

Appendix 1: Policy Development Framework

Element	Descriptor
Introduction/ Purpose	An introduction to the policy could combine the mission of the local district with the desire to provide equity for all individuals who visit the campus.
Definitions	Brief policies define service animals and emotional support animals, while lengthier policies may also include definition of pets, handlers, trainers, etc. These definitions may include characteristics and examples to clearly delineate each type of animal. PK–12 leaders are encouraged to use the definition from the Americans with Disabilities Act (ADA). Emotional support animals, regardless of permission to be on campus, should be defined and qualified. Clear definitions are designed to prevent ambiguity between animals that are and are not allowed on campus. Districts may wish to consider circumstances related to approval (i.e., reasonableness) of miniature horses as service animals. Depending on local need, leaders may wish to consider therapy dog and companion animal definitions, characteristics, and allowance on campus. For all animals allowed on campus, districts should also establish grievance/ removal policies for each type of animal.
Inquiries	According to the ADA, there are only two questions that organizations are allowed to ask about an animal. *Is the animal required because of a disability?* *What work or tasks has the animal been trained to perform?* The first is a *yes/no* question, and the second is only asked if the response to the first question is *yes*. School policy should include these questions. Leaders should also consider how this information (i.e., the only two allowable questions) will be disseminated to all employees to avoid illegal interrogations.
Training	According to the ADA, service animals are not required to be professionally trained. Handlers may train their own service animals.
Registration	There is no requirement for federal registration of service animals, and there is no requirement for an animal to be identified by a vest, leash, or collar. Registrations and identifying paraphernalia are voluntary and sold as commercial products. However, registration within the district/ school is recommended (see District Registration below).
Handling	Service animals must be under the control of their handler at all times by a physical device or other means of control. A leash, harness, or tether is required except in cases where the person's disability and/or the animal's work performance prevents using such devices. In these instances, the handler must maintain control by using voice commands, signaling, or other effective controls.
Local requirements	State and local public health and animal control requirements apply to service animals. Leaders are encouraged to inquire about local rules and regulations from governing bodies and look to local institutes of higher education policies, which may have included local requirements.

(continued)

Element	Descriptor
District registration	Local districts may wish to require service animals be registered with an oversight body within the school/district (e.g., student services, nursing services) solely for the purposes of communication to impacted stakeholders, coordination with individuals who have other health concerns (e.g., allergies), memos for understanding describing roles and responsibilities (e.g., waste removal, cleanliness of the dog), and/or tracking adherence to local requirements (e.g., annual immunizations). However, failure to register cannot be used as a criterion to disallow a service animal.
Family notification	Local leaders may consider the notification of parents when a service animal is being used in their student's classroom and/or school. If a child has an unreported allergy or severe fear, parents and leaders can communicate and find reasonable solutions for all parties involved. However, fears and allergies have been specifically identified as reasons that cannot be cause to exclude a service animal.
Behavior	Service animals can be removed from public facilities when their handler does not maintain control or fails to take corrective action to maintain control and/or if the animal is not housebroken.
Cleanliness	Districts may consider expectations for waste management and cleanliness. Service animals should be clean, well groomed, and free of pests such as fleas and ticks. Districts that incur pest control expenses above and beyond typical day-to-day operational requirements may consider billing these expenses to the handler. An area of the grounds should be designated for elimination, and the district should decide if solid waste cleanup will be the responsibility of the handler or part of the custodian's day-to-day responsibilities or assigned to another designee. The odor, noise, behavior, and waste of a service animal should not create an unreasonable disruption of the learning environment.
Grievances	Districts should consider the logistics of handling grievances. Decisions of timeliness, confidentiality, resolutions, and notification of involved parties should be considered. This section could also include viable reasons for removal (i.e., examples of policy violations).

APPENDIX: SAMPLE SERVICE DOG LETTER TO PARENTS

Dear Parents,

The Americans with Disabilities Act of 1990 defines service dogs as dogs that are trained to perform a specific, disability-related task so that the individual can fully participate in the major functions of life. Sometimes it also allows for a miniature horse to serve. I am writing to let you know that our campus regularly has at least one service animal.

If your student has a health concern that could be negatively affected, please contact the [administrative office] at [phone number] so that we can discuss accommodations.

We ask that you help us to teach our students how to behave when encountering a dog that is working by following these guidelines:

Do

- Ask before petting any animal
- Pet gently along the back toward the tail
- Look at the dog's tail (wagging means I'm happy; tail between my legs means that I am worried)
- Give the dog and person the right of way
- Try to ignore the dog as much as possible so she or he can work

Don't

- Shout, whistle, or make loud noises
- Get too close too quickly
- Touch without asking
- Offer food or drinks to the dog
- Be surprised if you are not allowed to pet the dog
- Ask specifics about the person's disability

Thank you for supporting and welcoming all members of the community to our campus!

Sincerely,
[Principal]

CHAPTER 10

ADDRESSING AND REMEDIATING SERVICE DOG ISSUES

To err is human—to forgive is canine.
—Author Unknown

> **ADVANCED ORGANIZER**
>
> Upon completing this chapter, you will be able to:
> - recognize retraining and control issues;
> - describe the purpose and content of a remediation plan;
> - identify reasons service animals can be asked to leave a facility;
> - determine ways to document control and specific criteria be met such as passing the AKC Canine Good Citizen's Test or Public Access Test;
> - decipher if and when to employ a service dog coach or use an alternative handler (i.e., parent or aide) if the child is unable to control the animal; and
> - understand species- and breed-specific behaviors and how they impact the animal's behavior.

SERVICES ANIMALS ARE NOT PERFECT. This may be a surprising statement; however, it is an important point to understand. Not all service animals respond correctly in all situations. Much like when technology fails or wheelchairs break down, a service animal may not perform to criteria in every situation. The reasons for this breakdown may vary. A service animal may not be fully prepared for its duties, or the environment may be one of overstimulation and unpredictability. Additionally, a handler may not be attending to the dog, may be sending mixed signals, or may not be maintaining training criteria. Finally, the animal may not feel well and may no longer be physically capable of performing a task. There are many reasons why things might not go as we planned.

When mistakes occur, the handler and people affected by the service animal must evaluate the impact of the error. Some errors are honest mistakes or can be easily fixed quickly with minor redirection or through understanding the context of the environment. Other errors may be chronic and require retraining to ensure the safety of the animal, handler, and other people in the setting without removing the service animal. In extreme cases when a handler cannot control a service animal or the animal is exhibiting behavior perceived as dangerous or unsanitary (e.g., lunging, defecating, or urinating), service animals can be removed from a setting temporarily or permanently.

The purpose of this chapter is to present options for addressing problems with service animals in the school setting. Legal remedies involving service animals in schools are provided in chapter 3. The focus of this chapter is to provide practical guidelines for addressing and remediating issues. Information is presented in a proactive to reactive format. First, we present solutions designed to prevent problems, including behavioral expectations for service animals. Next, we discuss practical suggestions for addressing minor problems within the school setting, such as identifying causes for misbehavior and retraining options. Finally, we address issues meeting the criteria for removing a service animal from the school and potential plans for reentry and retraining issues and resources, such as the development of a remediation plan for the animal or handler. We also provide sources for documenting control.

PROACTIVE PROBLEM SOLVING

Understanding Service Animal Expectations

A popular expression involving service animals is they are not identified so much through the vest as they are through behavior. Service animals are expected to possess some common characteristics suitable to working with their handlers with disabilities in public. Understanding behavioral and temperamental characteristics expected of a service animal is a fundamental component in preventing problems. This understanding is especially important for people selecting and training their own service animals. It provides criteria for selecting appropriate animals (e.g., temperament and physical aspects) and a foundation for readiness (e.g., basic obedience skills are required).

Service animals are held to high expectations. It is important to note that not every animal is suited for this type of work. It is estimated that 50 to 70 percent of potential service dog candidates do not make the cut (Duffy & Serpell, 2012). Hereditary diseases and behavioral problems are the most common reasons for a dog to be released from a training program (Wahl et al., 2008). As a result, careful selection is a must, and a realization that not all animals will succeed is an important mindset when training or working with a newly acquired service animal. A proactive problem-solving approach is to objectively assess if the animal possesses the characteristics needed to be a service animal prior to using them in public. Problems may arise when selecting a potential dog that is a wonderful companion and family pet but does not possess the expected qualities for a service animal working in public. Additionally, a suitable animal may have health issues preventing its effective use as a service animal. In the following section, we review criteria expected of potential service dogs.

Service Dog Criteria

A potential service dog must possess an even, stable temperament. The service dog should be people-oriented and handler-focused. It should be biddable and have a desire to please. It should have the ability to focus and not be distracted by an environmental stimulus such as loud noises, sudden movements, or aggressive behaviors from people or other animals. The service dog should consistently react in a calm and controlled manner regardless of the distractions. The dog should be confident and not display excessive anxiety. The dog should not display excessive reactivity (i.e., responding disproportionately to an event or circumstance when unprovoked) or aggression of any kind (Batt et al., 2008; Grace, 2019).

Service dogs should be trained not to respond to aggression from other animals in order to continually serve their handlers. This trait can be problematic if the service animal encounters untrained pets, emotional support animals, or fake service dogs that are not screened or prepared for the environmental stressors and react inappropriately with the service animal. The impact of these negative encounters can result in the service animal needing extensive retraining or being retired from service (Grace, 2019). Likewise, service animals should not be overly protective of their handlers. Children using a service animal interact with other students and may require assistance from adults who will touch or reposition them. As a result, a service dog must allow other people to approach their handler. For example, if a child with a physical disability falls out of wheelchair and needs assistance, the service dog should not block a person approaching to help (The Dog Training Secret, n.d.).

Service dogs should also master basic obedience skills. These skills include performing commands such as sit, down, and heel and staying in a designated position. The dog must be able to maintain a position over time in a small space such as under a table or in a seat well. The dog should reliably come to its handler when called. The dog should walk on a leash without pulling. The designated side or area for leash walking is dictated by the handler's needs. Dogs may be on the right or left, follow closely behind the handler in tight spaces, or work in front or block the handler slightly in crowds. A service dog should not leave its handler to greet people or investigate distractions, should not sniff or eat food or other desirable items, and should be reliably quiet and not vocalize (e.g., bark, whine, grumble, or growl) unless it is a part of a required task (Grace, 2019).

Health Issues

In addition to possessing an appropriate temperament and obedience skills, a service dog must be physically capable of performing designated tasks. A service dog may not follow a command or not react appropriately due to a health issue. Each breed of dog has its own particular health concerns. Dogs with degenerative joint disease, such as hip or elbow dysplasia, and spinal cord issues, such as degenerative disc diseases, can experience difficulty performing balance or pulling tasks requiring weight-bearing or resistance. The shoulder, hip, and lower back areas are typically used in these tasks. Similarly, a dog with congenital heart disease, Lyme disease, or thyroid issues may tire easily and not have the endurance to work for long periods. Age-related issues should be considered. Older dogs are prone to arthritis and vision issues such as cataracts, progressive retinal atrophy (PRA), or nuclear sclerosis. Symptoms of cancer, both subtle and obvious, can impact an animal's performance.

Implications of Service Dog Expectations

The list of expectations is important to consider. They provide an overall guide to selecting an appropriate service animal for self-training or evaluating the performance of the service dog in public. Although this list is intended to prevent problems, it paradoxically can create issues for service dog handlers. One such issue is perfectionism. Handlers feel their service dog needs to perform perfectly in public. Many service dog teams do; however, mistakes happen, particularly with new handler/service dog teams. An additional, compounding issue is legitimacy. Handlers with invisible disabilities are particularly prone to this issue. The legitimacy of the service animal is called into question when in public because they do not have an obvious disability (Mills, 2017). The presence of fake service dogs that behave inappropriately intensifies the scrutiny. As a result, handlers can put unreasonable expectations on themselves and their dogs to be flawless. Handlers may be concerned that an off day or a small mistake could make maintaining access to schools, buildings, and businesses more difficult (Pierce, 2018).

ADDRESSING MINOR PROBLEMS

If an occasional mistake occurs, acknowledge it, apologize to those involved, and reflect on it (Morris, 2015). If the error is due to an unusual or unexpected event, note the stimulus and acknowledge that it may be a possible trigger. However, do not dwell on it if it does not become a pattern. I experienced a tangential example of such an experience at a dog obedience trial in a large venue also hosting a cheerleading competition. A group of young, enthusiastic cheerleaders shaking pom-poms surrounded the competition ring during our performance. The young Labrador retriever being shown lost focus yearning to interact with the young girls and play with the pom-poms. Although the dog's performance was diminished, I learned the dog required more distraction training in dealing with children and moving objects resembling dog toys.

If errors occur on a consistent basis in related situations, a more thorough analysis is needed, and retraining may be required. Consider the following scenario: A young service dog periodically leaves its handler's side in public and jumps on a person who is approaching and greets the person by putting its paws on the person's chest and licking their face. The handler can address the situation at the moment by redirecting the service dog in a clear and positive manner to focus on them and return to the desired position (e.g., sitting or standing at the handler's side). Next, the handler should apologize to the person who received the unexpected greeting and acknowledge the error. Last, the handler should reflect on the error. In this case, the dog left their position without permission, put its paws on a person's chest, and licked their face.

Potential causes for this behavior could be a lack of behavioral criteria. The handler may allow the service dog to greet people within their inner social circle by jumping up on them and licking their face. The dog potentially receives positive reinforcement for these fun, interactive encounters. If this is the case, the dog may not fully understand where and when appropriate greeting behavior is expected. The handler may need to reconsider the utility of the paws on chest and face licking greeting behavior and determine if it should be allowed within the home. If the behavior is not part of a task needed by the handler with a disability, it should not be permitted within the home environment. Consistent expectations for greetings across settings should be maintained to allow the dog to perform consistently in all settings, including in public. Consistent, positive practice is required. Dogs do not generalize behaviors easily. Dogs tend to revert to highly reinforced behavior when stressed. Reinforcing proper greetings across settings will help alleviate problems in distracting situations.

If the handler chooses to allow paws on chest as a greeting within the home setting, a clear home greeting routine must be developed and maintained. The dog should be expected to maintain the criteria for the public greeting by remaining in place. The handler can then cue the dog that the task is complete. Some trainers use release words such as "OK," "All done," or "That'll do" to indicate the dog has finished performing the task and they may stop; others use words not likely to occur within conversation (such as "pop") to avoid mistakenly releasing the dog. Response to these release words must be directly taught. Next, the handler can teach explicitly a command for greeting people in the home environment (such as "Go say hello") that allows a dog to approach a person for petting. A clear criterion for home greeting behavior should be established and reinforced. For example, the dog may be permitted to move gently toward a person for petting but cannot remove any paws from the ground (e.g., four on the floor command) or lick the person's face. The handler must be prepared to call the dog from a person if the dog's greeting becomes overzealous. The handler should continue to monitor if greeting behavior is an issue in public. If errors continue to occur, the public greeting behavior routine should be continued to be reinforced across all settings and the use of the home greeting routine should be reassessed or discontinued.

In addition to evaluating the service dog's performance, be aware that the source of the behavior problem may be at the other end of the leash as well. Service dog handlers must maintain criteria for specific behaviors and reinforcement schedules for a service animal to be consistent. Behavior drift happens. Over time, handlers inadvertently can relax behavior standards and expect behaviors rather than occasionally reinforcing them. Keep in mind that not all service dog handlers have animal training experience. Some handlers are learning to interact with the service dog for the first time as they are learning to implement basic animal training techniques. Although many professional service dog training facilities offer transition support when a handler initially acquires a service animal, errors occur when learning new skills. Trainers from professional organizations can offer ongoing support. In addition, trainers with experience in preparing dogs can provide individualized coaching to assist handlers in working through specific issues. As a caveat, the service dog training industry is not regulated. Trainers do not have to obtain licensure or complete required courses. Licensure and continuing education are optional. Be sure to carefully select a trainer when working through an issue.

Many service errors can be avoided by understanding behaviors expected of service animals and recognizing sources of error (i.e., service animal, handler, or environment). Minor errors can be remediated if they are recognized, acknowledged, and addressed. Some retraining may be necessary. Major difficulties can occur when minor issues are not noticed or remediated. These small issues culminate into larger problems resulting in a service animal acting inappropriately and the handler not taking effective action to control them. This culmination can be compared to the formation of a spider's web. Small strands form from various directions and are hardly noticeable at first. For service animals and handlers, these strands are unrecognized animal, handler, and environmental issues. Yet, once the web is formed, the issues become noticeable and impactful, much like a fully formed web.

MAJOR ISSUES: LOSS OF CONTROL AND REMOVAL

A service animal is required to be under the control of its handler at all times. Major issues arise when the service animal is perceived as out of control. Control encompasses regulating bodily functions (i.e., reliably housebroken), governing behavior impulses (i.e., appropriate behavior in a stressful situation), and/or coping with stress or pressure by remaining calm (e.g., not responding to an aggressive animal or adapting to crowds and small spaces). Service animals that are unable to regulate their bodily functions or demonstrate impulsive behavior (e.g., pulling, barking, or leaving the handler) or stress reactions (e.g., barking, growling, lunging, or snapping) are perceived to be out of control. During these situations, the handler is expected to assist the service animal in regaining control. This expectation has serious implications. Service animals can be asked to leave a setting, such as a school or classroom, if they are not housebroken, if they are out of control and the handler does not take effective action to control it, or if the animal is behaving in a way that is threatening to the health and safety of other people. It is important to note that threats to health and safety must be based on actual risk, not speculation (ADA Coordinator Training Certification Program, 2018).

Determining Out-of-Control Behavior

Although the criteria for out-of-control behavior by a service animal appears to be clear and straightforward, it can be difficult to apply. Control can be contextual. It can be defined differently across environments and individuals; control is in the eye of the beholder. As a result, a person observing a service animal may perceive its behavior as problematic while the handler may view it as acceptable.

A first step in addressing perceived out-of-control behavior is to ensure the behavior is not part of a required task. Some tasks require a service animal to perform a behavior in a specific circumstance that can appear to be out of control. For example, some service dogs are trained to alert their handlers or another designated individual if a medical issue occurs. The alert behavior may take the form of nudging or bumping, whining, or barking. Other service animals are trained to leave their handlers and find a designated individual if a fall should occur. These service animals may run from their handler to a particular individual to seek assistance.

Addressing Out-of-Control Behavior

If the behavior is not due to a trained task required by the handler, it should be addressed. An overall framework for addressing major issues is to (a) clearly define expectations for the service animal in the school environment, (b) determine the source of the uncontrolled behavior, (c) develop an action plan, and (d) document control. Each of these steps is discussed in the following section.

Defining expectations. An initial step is to clearly define expectations for the service animal within the school setting. Behavior is contextual. Expectations vary according to the specific settings. Specific behavioral guidelines should be collaboratively developed for the classroom, hallways, cafeteria, laboratories, library, and gymnasium. Individuals from a variety of perspectives should be involved, including the handler, educators, administrators, and parents. A service coach or previous trainer can be involved to determine which specific skills need to be developed or retrained.

Determining the source of uncontrolled behavior. If a consensus regarding expectations of controlled behavior is determined and the behavior achieved, the remediation process ends at this point. If difficulties continue, further investigation is required to identify the source of the uncontrolled behavior. Various factors should be analyzed including environmental issues, handling skills, and service animals' readiness for public work. Environmental issues consist of physical, social, and time elements. Physical aspects impacting a service animal include flooring, space, desk arrangement, and opportunities for rest when needed. Each of these factors could trigger a potential issue. For example, if a service dog has recently slid on a slippery tile floor, it may avoid or refuse to walk on tile. Likewise, a service dog may refuse to settle under a student's desk. The dog may not be able to rest comfortably under the desk due to space constraints and become sore or fatigued. Likewise, other students may be inadvertently annoying the service dog by kicking it under the desk or distracting it, resulting in reactive behavior. Housebreaking accidents can happen if the instructional schedule does not coincide with the service animal's bodily needs. The handler may need to elicit the help of an aide to take the animal out to relieve during instructional time. This may be especially pertinent for older dogs who need more frequent breaks.

The training and handling skills of the person using the service animal should also be assessed. The service handler must possess the physical, cognitive, and animal-specific skills to manage the animal and maintain or regain control. If the handler is a child who cannot physically handle the animal, an aide can be assigned to assist with handling. The aides should be carefully selected. The same individuals should be used, if possible, to maintain consistency. They should have knowledge of the animal's verbal and nonverbal commands, reinforcement schedules, and physical needs. It is possible to exacerbate uncontrolled service animal behavior if consistency across commands, behavioral expectations, and schedules is not maintained.

In addition to assessing the environment and handler skills, the service animal's ability to perform in the school environment in general and ability to perform specific tasks required by the handler should be assessed. A trainer or service dog coach can help evaluate the animal's behavioral repertoire to determine if specific skills need to be remediated or trained. For example, a service dog may require additional training in impulse control in the presence of moving children or food in order to be able to perform to expectation in a classroom.

Develop an action plan. Once the sources for the behavioral difficulties are identified, an action plan for remediation can be developed. The plan should clearly identify the behavior to be addressed, if the service animal should be removed, the desired behavior to be achieved and how it will be monitored, who should be involved, and criteria for reinstatement. The handler and their family, education professionals, and trainers, if appropriate, can be involved in developing and monitoring the plan. The action plan can also include continuing education for the handler provided by a specific service dog organization and health screening for the animal. A school may also request documentation of controlled behavior.

Document control. Several behavioral assessments can be used to document if the service animal is under control or the handler can take effective actions to regain control. The Americans with Disabilities Act does not specify service animal training and certification requirements; however, school districts can request this documentation to reinstate a service animal.

The Canine Good Citizen (CGC) Test provides a general measure of the dog's and handler's behavior in the community. It was developed by the American Kennel Club (AKC) to assess basic manners and obedience and responsible dog ownership. It is used as an initial evaluation of the dog's and handler's behavior in public. The CGC is administered by a certified evaluator and consists of ten performance tests: (a) accepting a friendly stranger, (b) sitting politely for petting, (c) appearance and grooming, (d) walking on a loose leash,

(e) walking in a crowd, (f) sit and down on command and staying in place, (g) coming when called, (h) reaction to another dog, (i) reaction to distraction, and (j) supervised separation (American Kennel Club, n.d.). See table 10.1 for descriptions of each test.

The Public Access Test is used to determine a service dog's and handler's readiness to work in public. The test was developed by the International Association of Assistance Dog Partners (IAADP) and is designed to assess a set of minimum training standards for public access. The goal of the Public Access Test is to determine if a team is ready to work in public without trainer supervision. Evaluators must meet specific criteria and have adequate experience training dogs in order to administer the tests. The Public Access Test assesses both the handler's and dog's ability. According to the IAADP (n.d.), the handler must be able to (a) safely load and unload the dog from a vehicle; (b) enter a public place without losing control of the dog; (c) recover the leash if accidentally dropped; and (d) cope calmly with an access problem if an employee or customer questions the individual's right to bring a dog into that establishment. The dog must be able to (a) safely cross a parking lot, halt for traffic, and ignore distractions; (b) heel through narrow aisles; (c) hold a sit and stay when a shopping cart passes by or when a person stops to chat and pets the dog; (d) hold a down and stay when a child approaches and briefly pets the dog; (e) hold a sit and stay when someone drops food on the floor and hold a down and stay when someone sets a plate of food on the floor within eighteen inches of the dog, then removes it a minute later; (f) remain calm if someone else holds the leash while the handler moves twenty feet away; and (g) remain calm while another dog passes within six feet of the team during the test.

Once control is documented, a service animal may be reintegrated into the school setting. A trainer may accompany the team for a designated period of time to ensure training is generalizing into the school environment. The reader should refer to state law pertaining to service animals to determine the public access status of service dogs in training. School district permission may be required if service dogs in training are not entitled to public access.

Species-specific implications. The specific nature of the service animal used can impact performance as well. According to the Americans with Disabilities Act, only dogs and miniature horses can be used as service animals. The characteristics of each type of animal have implications for training and remediation. For example, dogs are by nature predators, while horses are prey animals, causing each species to respond differently when under similar situations. Dogs are likely to chase or pounce on fast-moving objects or people and move toward high-pitched sounds. These sounds can elicit quick, impulsive behaviors that are useful to predators catching prey but not appropriate for a public working environment such as a classroom or school building. In contrast, horses tend to flee from aversive stimuli rather than approach and encounter them. As a result, a miniature horse may be more likely than a dog to refuse or resist approaching something they perceive as threatening. The resistance or refusal can be problematic considering the size of a miniature horse. In addition, dogs tend to be highly social animals and seek human attention. Breeds typically used for service animal work, such as Labrador retrievers, golden retrievers, and German shepherds, have been specifically bred to engage with people. This high degree of social attraction may be the source of problematic behaviors. In contrast, horses tend to work for people rather than with them. As a result, they have a lower degree of social attraction (US Service Animals, n.d.).

SUMMARY

Learning to use a service animal is a developmental process. Handler and animal teams grow from experience and relationship. However, this growth process does not happen without errors. Some errors can be proactively prevented by recognizing expectations for service animals prior to working in public and attending to the animal's physical and health care needs. Minor problems typically involve simple mistakes; others are small patterns of errors. Handlers and trainers should recognize, acknowledge, and address these errors. Some retraining of the service animal or handler may be necessary.

More significant issues arise when a service animal is perceived to be out of control and the handler does not take effective action to address it. The service animal may be removed from the school setting until the issue is resolved. An overall approach for addressing major issues is to clearly define expectations for the service animal in the school environment, determine the source of the uncontrolled behavior, construct an action plan to develop appropriate behavior, and monitor progress to document control.

An important component of remediating errors is to honestly evaluate the service animal's performance and determine if the animal is adequately trained to work in public. Consider the service animal's health and well-being to ascertain if they are physically capable of working in the school environment. Decipher if the environment is appropriate for the animal or if other adaptations could be used. Evaluate the handler's ability to use the service animal and maintain control, and avoid expectations of handler perfectionism. Overall, it is important to accept that errors happen and to take steps to rectify them by examining the situation from both ends of the leash.

Table 10.1. AKC Canine Good Citizen's Test Items

Test	Purpose	Steps	Criteria
Accepting a Friendly Stranger	Dog allows a friendly stranger to approach and speak to handler in a natural, everyday situation.	Evaluator approaches dog and handler and greets handler in a friendly manner, ignoring the dog. Evaluator and handler shake hands and exchange pleasantries.	Dog must show no sign of resentment or shyness.
Sitting Politely for Petting	Dog allows a friendly stranger to touch it while with its handler.	Evaluator pets dog on the head and body. Handler may talk to dog throughout the exercise.	Dog may stand in place as it is petted and must not show shyness or resentment.
Appearance and Grooming	Dog welcomes being groomed and examined and permits someone other than the handler to do it.	Evaluator inspects dog to determine it is clean and groomed and softly combs or brushes dog, lightly examines ears, and gently picks up each front foot.	Dog accepts grooming but is not required to hold a specific position during examination.
Out for a Walk	Handler demonstrates control of the dog as it walks on a leash.	Dog and handler perform a right turn, a left turn, and an about turn with at least one stop in between and another at the end.	Dog is attentive to handler and responds to handler's movements and changes of direction.
Walking through a Crowd	Dog moves about politely in pedestrian traffic and is under control in public places.	Dog and handler walk around and pass close to at least 3 people	Dog may show some interest in people but should continue to walk with handler, without showing over-exuberance, shyness, or resentment.
Sit, Down, and Stay in Place	Dog responds to handler's commands to sit and down and remains in place.	Handler tells dog to sit and down (multiple commands permitted) and chooses a position for leaving dog in a stay and walks to the end of 20-foot-long line and returns to dog at a natural pace.	Dog must do sit and down on command. Dog must remain in the place in which it was left until evaluator instructs the handler to release dog.
Come When Called	Dog comes when called by the handler.	Handler walks 10 feet from dog, turns to face dog, and calls dog.	Dog returns directly to handler. Handler may encourage dog to come.
Reaction to Another Dog	Dog behaves politely around other dogs.	Two handlers and their dogs approach each other from approximately 20 feet, stop, shake hands, exchange pleasantries, and continue for about 10 feet.	Dogs should show no more than casual interest in each other. Neither dog should go to the other dog or its handler.

(continued)

Test	Purpose	Steps	Criteria
Reaction to Distraction	Dog is confident when faced with common distracting situations.	Evaluator presents two distractions (e.g., dropping a chair, dropping a crutch or cane, or person running by).	Dog may express natural interest and curiosity and/or may appear slightly startled but should not panic, try to run away, show aggressiveness, or bark.
Supervised Separation	Dog can be left with a trusted person and maintain training and good manners.	Handler goes out of sight for three minutes while evaluator or designee holds dog's leash. Evaluators may talk to dog but should not engage in excessive talking, petting, or management attempts.	Dog is not required to hold position but should not continually bark, whine, or pace unnecessarily or show no more than mild agitation or nervousness.

Source: https://www.akc.org/products-services/training-programs/canine-good-citizen/take-the-test/.

CHAPTER 11

SELF-ADVOCACY SKILLS

Don't play service dog police and harass disabled people. You can't see an invisible disability. Service dogs come in all sizes and breeds. No specific labels, vests, or IDs are required for service dogs. Encouraging suspicion makes outings harder for all service dog teams. Needing help with training or etiquette doesn't deserve bullying. Service dogs have to behave—but not like robots. A service dog team can have a bad day or need help. Harmful or very disruptive behavior deserves removal, whether it's a service dog or not.

—"Don't play service dog police" graphic, Psychiatric Service Dog Partners

ADVANCED ORGANIZER

Upon completing this chapter, you will be able to:

- understand common issues encountered by service dog handlers in schools and the community,
- identify access issues encountered by people with disabilities using service dogs and their families and how to counteract them,
- understand how the ADA definition of a service animal contributes to confusion about service animal status,
- recognize examples of unwanted attention experienced by service dog handlers and ways to avoid it,
- describe the unique needs of individuals with invisible disabilities using service animals and means to proactively address them,
- understand how application of service dog law leads to proactive self-advocacy,
- employ strategic handling skills to avoid difficulties with interactions, and
- understand the importance of utilizing service dog etiquette and how it supports the handler and the dog.

THE USE OF SERVICE ANIMALS can enhance the quality of life of a person with a disability. They provide support and increase independence by performing tasks that mitigate the impact of their handler's disability. Despite these benefits, using a service animal can create difficulties for a person and their family, requiring advocacy and public education. These issues include denial of access, questions about a service animal's legitimacy, presence of fake service animals, unwanted attention, and disruption to the service animal. The source of many of these issues is the public's misunderstanding of service animal law and how to interact with service animals. In response to these difficulties, service animal handlers and their families need to develop self-advocacy skills to address these situations. The purpose of this chapter is to describe problems people with disabilities and their families are likely to encounter when using a service animal in public and provide advocacy skills to assist them in confronting barriers. Information about service dog etiquette is also presented as a means to inform the public about service animal use and dispel common misconceptions. Lastly, recommendations for advocacy within the school context are discussed. Content is presented using a problem-solution format. We will discuss the problems service animal users typically encounter and offer proactive solutions for resolving them.

People with disabilities who use a service animal may be denied access to public places due to a misunderstanding of service dog law (see chapter 3). They are questioned about the legitimacy of their service dog, especially if they have an invisible disability, and may wrongly be required to prove their animal's status by showing an ID card or vest, which are not required under the Americans with Disabilities Act (ADA). Likewise, service animal handlers often are confronted with other difficulties: unwanted attention, requests to pet their dogs, and inquiries about the nature of their disabilities. The increasing presence of fake service dogs confounds the difficulties encountered by service dog handlers. Schools and businesses may be reluctant to provide access due to a negative experience from a fake service animal. Members of the public may confuse service dogs with other types of support dogs or animals that do not have public access rights under ADA. Unwanted attention, access difficulties, and illegitimate service dogs can cause anxiety to handlers when using the service animal (Mills, 2017; Nieforth et al., 2021; Schoenfeld-Tacher et al., 2017).

PROBLEMS ENCOUNTERED BY SERVICE DOG USERS

Service dog handlers encounter a variety of issues when using their service animal in public. Many of these issues are applicable to service animal use in schools as well. The majority of these issues are legally or experientially based. Members of the public and school personnel may lack knowledge of legal aspects of service dog identification, access, and vesting requirements (see chapter 3 for legal discussions). Additionally, they have limited experience interacting with service animals, resulting in a preconceived, stereotypical perception of service animals and a limited knowledge of service dog etiquette. Specific examples of issues are presented in the following section. The solutions involving self-advocacy are addressed later in the chapter.

Legal-Based Issues

A lack of legal knowledge regarding the use of service animals can create barriers for a student and family that require self-advocacy skills. Misinterpretation of federal and state service animal laws and their application is a common problem for people with disabilities and their families (Glenn et al., 2017). Members of the public are not aware of the definition of a service animal, terms used in the law to label them, and the extent of access provided (see chapter 3).

Access issues. "*No dogs allowed! Can't you read the sign on the front door!*" "*You can't bring that horse in the cafeteria. We serve food here!*" "*It can't be a service animal. It's not wearing a vest. Do you have an access card?*" These are examples of the many comments handlers hear when they attempt to enter a school with their service animals. A norm in the United States is to not allow pets into public places including schools. Many schools have strict policies regarding pets. People with disabilities are frequently confronted about service animal access when entering a new environment or encountering new people due to this norm. This is especially true for people with invisible disabilities (Mills, 2017). They are often denied access, asked to remove the service animals, or even confronted by school staff or bystanders.

Access issues are generally caused by ignorance or misunderstanding of access to service animals under ADA (1990). A person with a disability using a service animal is allowed the same access as any other person visiting the school for the same purpose. As a result, a student with a disability accompanied by a service animal is allowed the same access as other students in areas such as the classroom, restroom, and cafeteria.

Preconceived View of Service Animals

"*A miniature poodle? How is that little dog going to help you?*" "*Your dog has a blocky head like one of those rottweilers. It can't possibly be a service animal.*" Members of the public may mistakenly believe that only certain dog breeds can be service animals. Breeds like Labrador retrievers, golden retrievers, or German shepherd dogs were more frequently used as service animals in the past. Yet ADA does not restrict the breed of the dog used as a service animal (ADA Network, 2021). As the functions performed by service animals increase, the type of dog used to perform these duties varies. Some training facilities use mixed-breed dogs obtained from shelters or rescue organizations (Baughman et al., 2015; Walther et al., 2017). The size of the dog may vary according to the task. For example, smaller dogs can make effective alert dogs as psychiatric service dogs due to their portability. Agile, midsize dogs are effective hearing alert dogs because they can move quickly between the person and the source of sound. A larger breed could be valuable if the individual requires stability assistance. The source of this issue may be a lack of understanding of service animal tasks. A service animal must be specifically trained to perform tasks to mitigate the impact of the disability and must be needed by a person (28 CFR § 35.104). However, not all tasks are obvious to the public. For example, a larger service dog standing next to his student may not appear to be working but is actually present to support balance while walking. Likewise, a seizure alert animal may be gently nudging a student to alert them of an impending seizure.

Appearance of the service animal. *"That dog is not wearing a harness or vest; it can't be a service dog." "What does that dog do for you anyway? It doesn't even look like it's working."* In addition to preconceived notions about dog breeds used for service dog work and the nature of the task performed, members of the public may hold stereotypical views about the appearance of service animals. They may assume that all service animals are required to wear vests and harnesses when working in public. This issue often arises from a stereotypical representation of people with disabilities and service animals in the media and popular literature (ADA Network, 2021). Although stereotyped, ADA does not require that service animals wear vests or identifying tags.

Specialized equipment may be used to support the specific task the animal provides. Some guide dogs and miniature horses wear a harness with handles to support a student with limited vision or blindness with orientation and mobility. Other service animals who provide support with balance or blood sugar or seizure detection may not require specialized equipment. The type of lead, vest, or harness used must match the handler's fine motor ability. It may be difficult for some handlers, especially children, to independently attach a harness to a dog; therefore, a simple flat snap collar with a leash may be used.

Legitimacy of the service animal questioned. *"You don't look like you have a disability. Why do you really need a service dog?"* The legitimacy of a service animal is often called into question, especially for people with an invisible disability. The source of these issues is a misunderstanding of the definition of a disability under ADA. A disability is defined as a physical or mental impairment that substantially limits one or more life activities such as seeing, hearing, speaking, walking, eating, lifting, breathing, reading, concentrating, and thinking (28 CFR § 35.108). Note that some of the limitations are not directly observable. The only overt indication of the disability might be the presence of the service animal. As a result, the legitimacy of the service dog may be called into question because the handler does not *appear* to have a disability. People with invisible disabilities are questioned about the legitimacy of their service animal when in public on a regular basis. For example, Mills (2017) found that 77 percent of service dog handlers with invisible disability surveyed indicated the legitimacy of their service dog was questioned, while approximately 67 percent experienced discrimination daily.

Confusion with other types of support dogs. *"Look, kids, there's a therapy dog! Let's go say hello." "What a beautiful dog! We could use some emotional support right now. Can we pet him?"* The use of support animals has increased in the US over the past few decades (Rothstein, 2018; Walther et al., 2017). As knowledge spreads of the human-animal bond and its benefits to various populations, animals, particularly dogs, are used for a variety of reasons, including emotional support, stress release, recreational visits, and educational interventions like therapy dog reading programs. The increase in function has led to a familiarity and interaction with support dogs. Members of the public are likely to approach a service dog, assuming it is performing a therapeutic or recreational function, rather than avoiding it so it can work. Additionally, the presence of support animals with various functions and titles can make it difficult to determine their status and function. Not all animals with a specific title meet the ADA definition of service animals. Members of the public may have difficulty making this distinction. They may deny access to a legitimate service animal or allow unwarranted access to a support dog or an untrained pet, potentially putting the public and animal at risk because the animal is not prepared to handle the environment.

Fake service animals. As support animals become more prevalent in society, allegations of misrepresentation or fraudulent representation of animals as assistance animals have increased as well. Some owners will identify their pets as service animals in order to gain access to specific environments, such as schools, that have strict pet policies. This same legal ambiguity leading to difficulty determining the legitimacy of a service dog also contributes to the presence of fake service animals, especially service dogs.

Inconsistent terms are used in federal, state, and local law, as well as by the public; the lack of standardized certification and identification requirements for these animals also makes it difficult for the public to determine an animal's role or job (Parenti et al., 2013). For instance, the identification requirements for therapy animals are stricter and more overt than for service animals. Several therapy dog organizations require animals to wear identifying vests and present identification cards when entering a building, while ADA does not require this type of documentation. This confusion paves the way for misrepresentation of pets as assistance animals in order to gain illegitimate benefits, thereby increasing skepticism and scrutiny of legitimate assistance animals. Although some states are passing laws against fraudulent misrepresentation of a service animal, public confusion and the lack of a standardized certification process make these laws difficult to enforce (Schoenfeld-Tacher et al., 2017).

Interaction-Based Issues

In addition to encountering legal-based barriers, people using service animals face etiquette-based issues as well. Members of the public may lack experience and knowledge of how to interact with service animals, putting the handler in uncomfortable social situations, interfering with the animal's function, and potentially putting the handler at risk. These issues include unwanted attention, interfering with the work of the service animal, and unrealistic expectations of the animal's behavior.

Unwanted attention. *"Is that a golden lab? He is so beautiful! Where did you get him? What's it like to live with a service dog? Can I pet him?" "Hey, Kathy, do you see that service dog over there? Watch how he's helping that girl in the wheelchair."* Handlers often receive unwanted attention when they are accompanied by their service animals. All too often, people stop to talk to them about their service animals, request to pet the animal, or draw unwanted focus upon them by staring at them or following them. These situations can be detrimental to the animal and the handler. An unwanted approach or touch can startle an animal while it is working and cause injury to it and/or the handler, and the injury may not be visible. For example, a guide dog may lose focus when unexpectedly approached and cause the handler to stumble. Animals trained to assist with balance are taught to assume a specific position and tighten specific muscles before the handler puts weight on them. An unexpected distraction could cause the animal to move or relax during the balancing task, injuring them and possibly contributing to a handler fall. Unwanted attention can be particularly prevalent in school situations. Children are attracted to dogs and tend to respond with quick approaches, excited voices, and a desire to interact.

This unwanted attention has several consequences. First, people may focus exclusively on the service animal and not interact directly with the child. Second, the handler may be concerned about being perceived negatively when they have to advocate for their dog. Because people tend not to understand how to interact appropriately with service animals, handlers are often characterized as demanding or rude for protecting their legal rights or safety and have reported feeling unreasonable when expecting strangers not to talk to, bark at, or call their dog (Pierce, 2018).

Unrealistic expectations of service animals. *"That dog is nudging his owner and whining. That can't be a service dog! I thought they were supposed to be perfectly behaved!" "Look, that boy is asking the service dog to step off the curb, and it won't go. Apparently, it needs more training."* Service dogs are expected to be well behaved, and handlers may feel the pressure to maintain that image, even when the service animal is performing a trained task for them. Some tasks may look like inappropriate behavior, such as nudging a handler, but in fact are means of alerting the handler of a task-trained event; for example, an impending seizure for a handler with a seizure disorder or a person approaching from behind for a person with post-traumatic stress disorder. Other service animals are taught purposeful disobedience. For example, a guide animal can be taught not to follow a command such as stepping into the street if they perceive traffic or other threats. Some handlers have avoided taking their service animal out in public due to these unrealistic expectations (Mills, 2017). This may be especially true in a school setting in which the family and student feel the service animal is not welcome and is held to unreasonably high expectations. Administrators can help alleviate these issues by providing thorough training to their staff and students (see chapter 9).

SELF-ADVOCACY TECHNIQUES

The solution for many of the above stated barriers can be achieved through self-advocacy. Major elements of self-advocacy include education, attitude, and preparation. In regard to service animal use, this includes knowledge of service dog laws, maintaining a calm and confident attitude when confronted, being mentally prepared to respond, and taking proactive steps to prevent issues. In the following section, we present suggestions for addressing legal and etiquette issues as well as proactively preparing for using service animals in schools.

Legal Self-Advocacy

An important first step in legal self-advocacy is to know the law. Be familiar with the federal definition of a service animal. According to the Americans with Disabilities Act (ADA), a service animal must be individually trained to perform tasks for the benefit of an individual with a disability, including a physical, sensory, psychiatric, intellectual, or other mental disability (28 CFR §

35.104). The animal must perform a task that a person with a disability could not perform independently and that mitigates the disability (i.e., makes the disability less severe, serious, or painful). Also know your state and local laws (see Wisch, 2021). Although ADA provides the overall standard for service animals, state and local laws can provide additional protections and these levels of protection can vary. For example, some states provide access to service dogs in training while other states do not. Additionally, some states do not provide protection to psychiatric service animals (Parenti et al., 2013).

In addition to acquiring legal knowledge, be prepared to share it when confronted. In other words, consider situations where this information will be beneficial and make a plan. Write a short, well-written paragraph explaining your rights as a person with a disability or a parent of a child partnered with a service animal and carry it with you. Refer to your written explanation when needed (Service Dog Central, 2020). You can also memorize your explanation and practice reciting it so that you can say it effortlessly when confronted. See the end of this chapter for an example statement of rights. It is also possible to purchase a laminated card containing this information from various organizations that you can show members of the public if public speaking is an issue.

Along with knowing the definition, be prepared to share task-related information. ADA does not directly define specific trained tasks but mandates they must be needed to lessen the impact of the disability. The only thing the ADA clearly states is that *comfort* is not a task (Pierce, 2018). According to ADA, you can be asked what work or tasks the animal is trained to perform for you (29 CFR § 38.16(f)). Be prepared to clearly articulate these tasks. Write out examples and practice them so you can state them under pressure. Remember that you are not required to demonstrate the tasks. Task knowledge is particularly important for people with invisible disabilities, especially those using a psychiatric service dog. As previously noted, ADA does not recognize comfort as a task. As a result, for a person with a psychiatric service dog, the response to an inquiry about the task should make the distinction between this animal and an emotional support animal that provides comfort only (Glenn at al., 2017). The details of the task that you provide do not need to include or reveal your disability.

In addition to knowing your rights under ADA, understand its practical application and the application of Section 504 of the Rehabilitation Act (see chapter 3). ADA and Section 504 are civil rights legislation. They provide the person with a disability using a service animal to equal access to programs and services and prevent discrimination. Equal access means that a person with a disability using a service animal receives the same access a person without a disability has in the same situation (28 CFR § 35.136(g)). It does not guarantee specialized access and services. The extent of access can vary depending on your role and the purpose of the visit. In terms of schooling, a child with a disability using a service animal is provided the same access to areas in the school at the same time as any other student. (See chapter 6 for more information about roles and access.) Likewise, a service animal only receives equal access when accompanying the person with a disability for which it is trained. A service animal who is not accompanied by the person with a disability for whom it was trained (i.e., a parent, friend, or other family member is with the animal) does not receive equal access or other ADA/Section 504 protections because it is not working. This is a fine yet important distinction. Consider a parallel situation in which a person with a disability uses a handicapped placard on their car to access handicapped parking. They are entitled to handicapped parking if they are in the car. However, if a family member or friend uses the car with the placard displayed, they are not entitled to handicapped parking despite the placard because they do not have a disability.

Along with understanding ADA application, know what constitutes a violation and what to do when it occurs. ADA violations occur when a person with a service animal is denied access equal to a person without a disability in the same situation. Remember that ADA is a civil rights law that can only be enforced by the court. Police are not empowered to enforce it. Begin by using your legal knowledge and rehearsed statement to inform the entity that you are a person with a disability. Explain that you are a person with a disability accompanied by a trained service dog, and ADA permits people with disabilities to be accompanied by their trained service dog even in places where pets are generally not allowed. Maintain your composure. Attitude is a key component in self-advocacy. Remain calm and confident when confronted. Many access issues can be resolved through a professional presentation (Service Dog Central, 2020).

In addition to legal knowledge, handlers can advocate for themselves by practicing strategic handling skills. Proactive planning and preparation are fundamental aspects of self-advocacy. The service animal should be well groomed and clean. Some handlers may choose to use a type of cape or vest on their service animals to clearly identify them. Although not required by ADA, members of the public easily recognize this form of marking for a service dog. In addition, the animal should appear to be well behaved and under control. As a handler, develop and practice some essential control commands to use in stressful situations such as sitting, lying down, and waiting in place. Make these commands part of a routine so they can be used quickly and efficiently when needed. For example, one handler uses a settle command in which the dog lies down, rolls toward one hip, and puts its chin on the ground in a resting position. This position was practiced and highly reinforced in a variety of situations, allowing it to become the default behavior during stressful situations while giving the appearance to others that the dog is under control.

Interaction Self-Advocacy

In addition to gaining legal knowledge and learning to handle confrontations regarding access, service animal handlers may encounter difficulties related to public interactions. Members of the public have limited understanding of how to interact with service animals, resulting in unwanted attention, interference with the work of the service animals, and unrealistic expectations of the animal's behavior (Nieforth et al., 2021). Service dog handlers can proactively address these issues. For example, when using a service animal in public, move quickly and with intent to avoid interruptions. Objects such as a backpack or bags can help to create space when maneuvering through a crowd or in a school hallway. If physical space is needed due to anxiety or a disability such as autism, the service animal can be taught blocking tasks, such as putting themselves between their handler and an approaching person or alerting the handler with a bark or nudge to someone from behind. If approached and asked about their service animals, handlers should provide quick and concise answers. Do not feel compelled to explain the situation or tell your story. Consider practicing these answers in advance as needed (Service Dog Central, 2020).

Service animal etiquette. Public knowledge of service animal etiquette can ease stress and distraction during interactions. Examples of service dog etiquette include not touching or feeding the animal without permission, not interfering with the dog's work, talking directly to the handler and not the dog, and providing adequate space. As a handler or family member, be prepared to explain to and request service animal etiquette from members of the public. Patience and understanding are often required as few people have direct experience with service dogs (Glenn at al., 2017). Yet service animal users can often feel burdened with teaching others service dog etiquette. Consider proactively requesting support from people and organizations regularly visited or people who regularly attend outings with the handler. For example, provide service animal etiquette materials to schools, agencies, or therapists a student may visit. Contact school administrators about conducting training regarding service animal etiquette for faculty, students, and staff, and suggest they especially include individuals like cafeteria workers who will encounter service animals in a setting in which food is also being served. Additionally, handlers might consider asking otherwise bystanders to assist with the advocacy in advance of being in situations where advocacy is needed. Again, consider having frank conversations with your acquaintances in advance and potentially practicing different scenarios together.

Addressing school issues. Discussions on service dog etiquette and legal rights often lead to other individuals stating their needs as well. Parents or administrators may be concerned about the impact of a service animal on children and staff with allergies or fear of dogs. However, the US Department of Justice, responsible for oversight of the ADA, specifically addresses these two instances as situations where a handler's rights cannot be denied (US Department of Justice, 2015). Disability awareness, an understanding of how a service animal assists with the disability, and knowledge of the animal's ability and needs can help navigate these situations by prioritizing essential skills, identifying areas of compromise, and recognizing service animal needs. Prioritize in advance the specific, essential tasks necessary for the service animal to perform their work and elements that cannot be changed in order for the service animal to successfully complete these tasks. Next, identify areas of compromise. Consider elements that might be altered within the given context but still allow for necessary assistance to be provided. Examples can include classroom seating, routes the service animal travels throughout the school, and where the service animal rests when not actively assisting its handler. Also recognize the service animal's abilities and needs when addressing issues. For example, when dealing with allergies and fear, proximity is an issue. If the handler knows the amount of space a service animal requires, optional positions in the classroom, and where and how the animal can settle (e.g., fit under a desk, lie next to the student or on a designated mat), routines for circulating around the classroom and avoiding exposure can be developed.

Advocating for the Whole Team

Service animals and their handlers work as teams. A unique aspect with service animal use is the dynamic relationship existing between the handler and animal. Much time and training has occurred to create trust and dependability within the relationship. As the handler, you rely on the animal's support, and your animal relies on you to ensure its overall well-being (Pierce, 2018). Replacing a service animal is a time-consuming, expensive, and emotional process (see chapter 5). As a result, the handler will need to advocate for their animal during interactions and consider the animal's needs. Animals may need periodic breaks and a quiet resting place when not working. Plan regular times for relief breaks during the school day, and scan the environment to potential hazards such as toxic substances or sharp surfaces. Periodically review your animal's stress level and physical health and maintain regular veterinary care.

Be aware of the presence of other animals in schools. The use of support animals, such as therapy dogs and emotional support animals, has increased in schools. Further, fraudulent representation of pets as assistance animals has climbed as well. Be vigilant. Not all of these animals are prepared for other animal interactions. Be prepared to ask for space or removal of the other animal if they impact your service animal or their ability to perform their work. Remove service animals from the situation if needed. Indicate that your dog does not need to meet or interact with other dogs and is presently working.

Protect your service animal's energy and time. Handlers may receive requests for their service animals to also work as therapy animals within a classroom. Consider these requests carefully and determine if they are in the animal's best interest and/or your best interest. In some cases, this dual role increases the animal's stress level because the roles are contradictory to the service animal's training. For example, some service animals are trained to focus exclusively on their handler and respond only to their handler's commands. They may become confused while in a dual role and not understand when to interact with others and when to be handler focused. Their performance may diminish due to confusion, and they may fatigue more quickly due to the increased workload.

SUMMARY

The use of service animals can enhance the quality of life of a person with a disability. They provide support and increasing independence by performing tasks that mitigate the impact of the handler's disability. Despite these benefits, using a service animal can create difficulties for a person and their families. The source of many of these issues is the public's misunderstanding of service animal law and how to interact with service animals.

Service animal handlers and their families can use self-advocacy skills to resolve these issues. Legal self-advocacy skills include being familiar with service dog law and how it is applied. Proactively preparing for questions about access and legitimacy will help diminish the negative impact of these interactions. Develop and rehearse statements summarizing the law and the tasks your animal provides. Practice remaining calm and confident when confronted. Create a positive presentation by maintaining the service animal's appearance and hygiene. Although not legally required, consider clearly identifying the service animal with a vest or cape to help the public recognize the animal's status.

In addition, prepare for difficulties related to public interactions. Many people do not know how to interact with service animals. Unwanted attention, interruptions, or confusion with other types of support animals is likely to occur. Move with intent and confidence in public, provide quick responses to inquiries, and create space if needed. Provide information on service dog etiquette to people in regularly visited environments.

Be prepared to address common issues such as allergies and fear of dogs. Prioritize specific, essential tasks necessary for the service animal to provide assistance and elements that cannot be changed. Identify areas of compromise and recognize the service animal's abilities and needs when addressing issues.

Advocate for the service animal. Understand the needs of the service animal. Identify potential hazards, plan for encounters with other animals, and determine appropriate actions if needed. Remove a service animal from a situation if it appears unsafe. Protect the service animal's energy and time by carefully considering the impact of additional tasks such as interacting with other students in class.

EXAMPLE STATEMENT OF RIGHTS

- *I am a person with a disability who uses a service dog. According to federal law (Americans with Disabilities Act), my service dog can accompany me in all areas where the public is allowed including areas in which food is served.*
- *You may ask me two questions about my service dog: (1) Is the dog a service animal required because of a disability? and (2) What work or task has the dog been trained to perform?*
- *You are not permitted to ask me about my disability, require medical documentation, require a special ID card or training documentation for the dog, or ask the dog to demonstrate its tasks. A person with a disability cannot be asked to remove his service animal unless the dog is out of control and the handler does not take effective action to control it or the dog is not housebroken.* (Service Dog Central, 2020)

CHAPTER 12

TRANSITION PLANNING FOR INDIVIDUALS WITH SERVICE ANIMALS

A canine partner in a service dog team is not a supportive device that just waits for a person in the office or at home. Well-trained service animals work most effectively when people help them maintain their skills and incorporate them into all aspects of daily activities. The animals live, play, and work with their partners. This means someone who is contemplating using a service dog for independence must be aware of the barriers and supports that are in all parts of their lives, including home, employment, healthcare, recreation, public accommodations, and transportation.

—Margaret K. Glenn et al., "Legislation and Other Legal Issues Relevant in Choosing to Partner with a Service Dog in the Workplace"

ADVANCED ORGANIZER

Upon completing this chapter, you will be able to:

- identify legal and procedural elements involved in the transition process;
- determine environmental, personal, and service animal factors related to the transition from school to the next environment;
- proactively identify demands of the next environment when transitioning with a service animal;
- identify issues specific to the workplace when using a service animal;
- identify the legal aspects of bringing a service dog to a place of employment or campus and determine sources of support;
- determine academic issues needed to be considered when bringing a service dog to campus, such as scheduling, classroom arrangement, and class type, and develop potential solutions to address them;
- recognize the residential issues involved when living with a service dog on campus;
- understand the social issues, both positive and negative, involved with using a service dog on campus; and
- learn service dog etiquette as it applies to the college environment.

STUDENTS WITH DISABILITIES using a service animal eventually become adults using a service animal in the community, including places of employment and college campuses. Although the inevitability of the transition is obvious, many components required to transfer environments are not. The complexity is compounded when the impact of a disability and the use of a service animal are added to the equation. Factors related to demands of the new employment or educational environment, the impact of disability, and the service animal must be considered. The purpose of this chapter is to present environmental, personal, and service animal factors related to transition from school to the next environment. We discuss transition to postsecondary, employment, and independent living environments. Prior to addressing these factors, we present legal requirements and procedures for transition.

WHAT IS TRANSITION?

Transition services are activities that prepare students with disabilities to move from school to postschool life. All students with a disability using a service animal can benefit from transition services, but not all students are entitled to transition services provided by the school. The extent of transition services provided depends upon the legal coverage afforded to the student. Transition services are not legally mandated for students with disabilities using a service animal who do not receive special education. Students not eligible for special education are protected under the Americans with Disabilities Act (ADA) and Section 504 of the Rehabilitation Act of 1973 (Section 504), civil rights legislation providing equal access and prohibiting discrimination based on disability. ADA and Section 504 do not mandate transition services. These laws protect people with disabilities throughout their life span and across environments. There is no specific transition point with their coverage.

In contrast, transition services are legally mandated for students using a service animal who receive special education services. These students are covered by the Individuals with Disabilities Education Act (IDEA), as well as ADA. IDEA is educational legislation guaranteeing a free appropriate public education and related services to students with disabilities from birth to twenty-one or high school graduation, whichever comes first. Once the student leaves the K–12 system, they are no longer covered by IDEA and transition to coverage under ADA alone; therefore, transition services are mandated by IDEA to prepare for this change. This legal distinction is important because it dictates the support students with disabilities and their families receive with the transition process. Families of students covered only by ADA must proactively initiate transition planning, identify support systems, and, if needed, coordinate services through local or state resources (e.g., Office of Vocational Rehabilitation or Center for Independent Living). Students covered by both IDEA and ADA receive more extensive support from the school. IDEA requires specific transition components to be included in a student's individualized education program (IEP).

IDEA Transition Components

For students covered by IDEA, transition planning involves the development and implementation of individualized and actionable services across academic, vocational, and community living domains. Transition services are defined by the Individuals with Disabilities Education Act (IDEA) of 2004 as a coordinated set of actions within a results-oriented process focused on improving academic and functional achievement of youth with a disability to facilitate their movement from school to postsecondary activities, including postsecondary education, vocational education, integrated employment (including supported employment), continuing and adult education, adult services, independent living, or community participation. Transition service planning is individualized, considering the student's strengths, preferences, and interests. Transition services are composed of specifically designed instruction, related services, community experiences, the development of employment and other postschool adult living objectives, and, when appropriate, the acquisition of daily living skills and functional vocational evaluation. The transition planning process should begin early. According to IDEA 2004, transition goals and services should be incorporated into the IEP during the year in which the student turns sixteen. Some states are more proactive, requiring transition planning to begin at age fourteen.

Transition and service animals. The transition process is more complex for students using a service animal. The unique needs of the student, service animal, and their dynamic working relationship must be juxtaposed with the demands of a new environment. Environmental, personal, and service dog factors must be considered. An ecological analysis is needed to identify challenges and barriers in the new environment, determine existing support, and create new supports required in employment, educational, or independent living situations. Personal factors include identifying individual strengths and needs of the handler based on the demands of the new environment, the impact of the disability and disability awareness, and the amount of personal support needed in the new environment.

Service animal factors involve generalization of existing tasks to a new environment, identifying new tasks, and providing any additional training required for the next environment. Animal-specific issues, such as care, storage, veterinary services, travel, unique stressors or hazards, and acclimation to a new environment, must be addressed. Strategic handling skills required in the new environment should be determined as well. In the following sections, we discuss the environmental, personal, service animal, and handling factors related to the transition to employment and continuing education.

TRANSITION TO EMPLOYMENT

Environmental Analysis

Successful transition from school to employment for a student with a disability using a service animal begins with an ecological analysis comparing the current environment to a potential employment setting. This analysis involves exploring all settings involved. Some environments, such as the workplace itself, are obvious targets; however, other environments involved in employment are not. These less obvious environments include transportation back and forth to work, the physical layout of the path needed to access the workspace (e.g., parking lots, entry doors, flooring, steps, elevator, furniture or equipment arrangement, etc.), and even changes in the home environment required for the handler to expediently prepare for work to ensure an on-time arrival. As a result, multiple settings must be examined to anticipate the tasks and skills required. The purpose of this analysis is to identify new or challenging tasks needed in the next environment and juxtapose them to the handler's current ability and the service animal's current skills. Development and transfer of these skills should be addressed early, while the student is still in high school, to help support acquisition of gainful employment.

Once skills required for the projected work environment are identified, the student's abilities must be considered. A potential work environment may present new physical or task-related challenges the student has not encountered in the school or home setting. Student strengths should be assessed to determine their level of independence and ability to circumvent challenges and perform specific tasks for which assistance from the service animal is required. Disability awareness is an important component in identifying these tasks. The student must understand the impact of their disability in the current setting and project it into the anticipated work-related environments to determine skills they can do independently, if current tasks performed by the service animal are applicable, and new tasks required.

Consider the following example. A student must use public transit, such as a bus or subway, to commute to a projected work site. Riding a bus or subway is similar to using school transportation, such as a van or bus. The student is able to board the van using the service dog for balance or mobility, and the dog is able to curl up in a seat well or under a seat. When using a school provided bus or van, a driver typically opens and closes the doors, and upon exit, traffic stops to allow students to cross a street. Subtle but important distinctions exist when using public transportation. Many forms of public transformation use automatic doors with sensors to remain open if a person is in the doorway. Most automatic doors do not detect the presence of a dog alone because it is too small or low to the ground. A service dog is at risk of being crushed by automatic doors if it is not walking next to its handler or the door is blocked by the handler. As a result, the handler and dog must walk through the automatic door side by side or in close proximity. The handler must ensure all parts of the dog and leash have passed through the door before it closes or use their body to block the doors to ensure the automatic door does not close on the dog. This same skill set can be generalized to elevators if they exist in a potential workplace. Further, when exiting a public bus, the dog and handler must detect oncoming traffic and automatically stop when traffic is approaching. If the handler is not able to detect traffic easily, a new traffic-sensing routine needs to be developed in which the service dog alerts or blocks the handler when seeing or hearing approaching traffic.

Service animal needs in the projected work environment also should be considered. Basic needs, such as access to a relief area or a quiet resting place when not working, should be contemplated. Projected hazards should be identified including machinery, toxins, or slippery floors. The fit between the service animal and the potential clientele served in the workplace should be considered. For example, children can be unpredictable, active, and overly interested in the service animal. Children also can make novel sounds such as high-pitched voices, squeals, and crying that are irritating to the service animal.

Some service animals may tire quickly when navigating crowds for long periods, and periodic rest breaks are needed. Effective handling skills are needed when working with certain elderly people who may be frail, experience balance issues requiring special equipment, and have thin skin susceptible to tears. I experienced a particular issue when training a Labrador retriever to work in a supported care setting: the use of tennis balls on the bottom of a walker's legs. The dog was interested in retrieving the tennis balls. Some special training on leaving tennis balls on command was needed because they were typically used in training as reinforcement in other situations.

In addition to an environmental analysis, the essential job functions of a projected occupation and its relationship to service animal use should be examined. Some students are able to perform the essential job functions without the explicit support of a service animal, while others need to determine how the service animal will support their job performance. For instance, a student with a physical disability using a wheelchair and service animal may perform essential functions for a sales position on a sales floor and only requires the service animal to support travel to and from work and transitions in and out of the chair at various points during the day, such as using the restroom. In contrast, a student with balance issues may require the dog to be present on the sales floor to support mobility.

Legal Knowledge and Self-Advocacy

In addition to determining environmental factors, personal factors, and service animal skills, knowledge of service animal law and its application in various environments related to job acquisition (e.g., employment, housing, travel) is important. The ability to actualize this knowledge through self-advocacy is essential as well.

Employment. Title I of the Americans with Disabilities Act (ADA) of 1990 prohibits employers from discriminating against qualified people with disabilities in job application procedures, hiring, firing, advancement, compensation, job training, and other terms, conditions, and privileges of employment. A qualified employee with a disability is a person who, with or without reasonable accommodation, can perform the essential functions of the job. Examples of reasonable accommodation include (a) making existing facilities used by employees readily accessible to and usable by persons with disabilities; (b) job restructuring, modifying work schedules, or reassignment to a vacant position; and (c) acquiring or modifying equipment or devices; adjusting or modifying examinations, training materials, or policies; and providing qualified readers or interpreters. Service animals are considered reasonable accommodations. A job applicant or employee is responsible for making the argument that a service animal meets the definition of a reasonable accommodation. As a result, students must understand the impact of their disability in a potential employment setting and how the tasks performed by the service animal mitigate the impact. However, responsibility also lays with the employer to be diligent in providing sufficient interactive opportunities to work through the request tasks (Glenn et al., 2017).

Interestingly, an employee with a disability may request accommodations for the service animal to allow it to safely perform its tasks (Glenn et al., 2017). This is analogous to making a work environment safe and accessible for a person using a wheelchair. In the case of *McDonald v. Department of Environmental Quality* 351 Mont. 243 (MONT. 2009), Bess, McDonald's service dog, continuously slipped and was injured due to slippery floors in the workplace. McDonald requested mats be put down on routes in which the service dog routinely traveled. The Department of Environmental Quality (DEQ) did not comply. McDonald filed a complaint and won. DEQ appealed to the Judicial District Count and won by arguing the mats were accommodating the service dog and not McDonald. Upon appeal, the State Supreme Court of Montana reversed the decision, indicating accommodations made to allow the service dog to perform needed tasks were essentially accommodating McDonald, the handler.

Housing. In addition to legal knowledge pertaining to the workplace, students using a service animal may also require legal knowledge pertaining to housing. A goal of obtaining gainful employment is to transition to independent living. Under ADA, service animals are not legally considered pets; therefore, they are not subject to pet rules or policies of housing providers such as size or weight restrictions, exclusion from specific common areas, or access restrictions to only a particular door or elevator. In addition, no pet deposits should be charged for service animals. State law and local or municipal governments can provide additional protection. As a result, the student should be aware of service dog law regarding housing in their particular community (Glenn et al., 2017).

Travel. Some employment positions require periodic travel to other locations or events such as sales meetings, supervision, or conference attendance. A student using a service animal may benefit from legal knowledge and access rights pertaining to air transportation, public transportation, and private vehicles such as hotel shuttles, taxis, and ride services (e.g., Uber, Lyft). Travel may also involve eating in restaurants and hotel stays. Legal knowledge and advocacy skills regarding public access in these settings are needed as well. Further information about service dog law and self-advocacy skills are presented in chapters 3 and 11 respectively.

Transition to employment may be an ultimate goal for many students using a service animal. Some students will transition directly into employment after high school; others will pursue postsecondary education in order to meet their career goals. Depending on their intent, students using service animals need to prepare for the college environment as well.

TRANSITION TO POSTSECONDARY EDUCATION

Transition from high school to college for a student using a service animal involves many of the same elements involved in transition to employment.

Environmental, personal, and service dog factors must be considered. However, the scope of these factors is distinctly different, especially for students who are planning to live on campus. All areas of life are impacted, including participating in academic life, living in the residence halls, and navigating the campus and classrooms. Like many college students, transition to college may be the first time a person with a service animal has assumed responsibility for many aspects of their lives. Students using service dogs not only need to address their own needs but the needs of their service animal. In addition, they often become ambassadors for service dog etiquette on campus as well. As a result, legal knowledge, self-advocacy, and problem-solving ability are necessary skills.

Bringing a Service Dog to College

Deciding to bring a service animal to college is a complex decision. Benefits, advantages, and challenges should all be considered. Benefits include the tasks and support the service animal provides to mitigate the person's disability in everyday life and in the college environment as determined by the environmental analysis. Consider if these tasks are most efficiently performed by the service animal or by other means, such as specialized equipment or accommodations.

The presence of a service animal offers distinct advantages during the transition to college. These advantages include a great sense of confidence and independence perceived by the handler, potential for increased social interaction on campus, and the constant companionship of a service animal especially if leaving home to attend college. These advantages may be counterbalanced by challenges, including the responsibility of caring for a service animal independently in a college environment. The time, care, and attention required by the service animal must be considered in all aspects of college life, not just while the animal is working.

Some colleges students with disabilities have reported feeling conflicted with time and social engagements when using a service animal in college. Not all friends may feel comfortable with the service animal. As a result, the animal may spend extended time alone when the handler is socializing with this friend. Not all social events are appropriate for service animals, such as concerts in which service animals may not be easily seen in a dark venue while curled under a seat or crowded events. Transport and expense of veterinary care and acquisition of supplies should be considered as well (Moldin, 2008). All these issues should be discussed prior to and during the transition to college to determine the optimal plan for each person and service animal team.

College-Specific Aspects of Transition

Requesting accommodations. Prior to arriving on campus, the student should notify their college's Office of Disabilities Services that they will be using a service dog on campus. Representatives from this office can help arrange class schedules and address housing issues if needed. The Office of Disability Services may provide the student with an accommodation letter indicating a service dog will accompany them to class and outlining any additional accommodations needed. If the person's disability is evident, typically no additional document for using a service dog is needed based on ADA implementation. If the disability is not evident, the college may request documentation for the service animals such as a letter from a doctor or psychiatrist documenting the presence of the disability. Not all campuses require students with service dogs to register with the Office of Disability Services if no other academic or access accommodations are needed. However, representatives from this office can provide valuable assistance and access to additional resources.

For students who have received services for special education under the Individuals with Disabilities Education Act in high school, the mandate for students to disclose and document their disability to receive accommodations in higher education is a key component in transition. During their time in public schools, IDEA mandates schools actively seek out students with disabilities, provide evaluations to determine eligibility, and provide services. When students with disabilities leave public schools and enter college, the IDEA coverage ends, and ADA applies. Under ADA, as in an employment situation, the person with a disability is responsible for notifying the college of their disability and requesting reasonable accommodations. Students should be made aware of this requirement during the transition and begin assembling needed documentation prior to attending college.

Housing. If a student is living on campus with a service animal, housing must be considered prior to arriving on campus. For example, a student will need a room large enough to accommodate a service animal, especially if it is a larger dog or miniature horse, and to store special supplies such as crates, beds, food, toys, and specialized equipment such as leashes and harnesses. Ideally, the room should have easy access to a relief area accessible at all hours. In some cases, a student may exit a dormitory during night hours through a convenient door near their room to the relief area but need to return to the main door to reenter the building due to security. A possible accommodation is to request a key and any security clearance for specific entrances in advance to allow for easy access during night hours.

The presence of a service animal may impact roommate selection. The roommate must be comfortable sharing space with a service animal. Allergies or fear of animals must be considered. In addition, the roommate must understand the role of the service animal is to provide support for the person with a disability and understand service animal etiquette. The service animal is not a pet or therapy animal. Depending on the circumstances, the roommate may be asked to not interact with the service animal unless directed to avoid distracting it from its work. Some students with service animals may prefer a single room to avoid the complexities of interacting with a roommate (Lalliss, 2019).

Scheduling issues. Class schedules must be considered when using a service animal. Breaks should be planned to allow the animal to relieve and rest. The nature of the class (lab versus lecture) must be considered to prepare the animal for the environment. In lecture classes, the service animal may need to sit still in a small space close to the handler for an extended time. In science labs, computer labs, or other classes requiring movement around the room, the service dog will be required to reposition often, navigate around specialized equipment, or stay on a mat in a corner of the room outside the path of constant movement (Ramp, 2020).

Students can alert professors in advance that a service animal will be attending class. Some professors will be comfortable and experienced with dealing with service animals. Others may need some guidance on service animal etiquette. The student can ask a professor to inform the class the service animal will be attending. The student also can request an opportunity to address service animal protocol with classmates during the initial class session. In some cases, students will be familiar with the presence of the animal, and no direction is needed. If the animal is used to alert conditions such as impending seizures or low blood sugar, the student may want to inform the professor or a designated student of procedures to follow if the dog alerts.

In addition to class schedules, students with service dogs must plan time for the dog to relax and exercise when not working. Play and informal walks can be an effective stress reliever for service dogs in particular. Students must learn to anticipate their service dog's need for rest and recuperation. Identify preferred activities that the dog and handler both enjoy, such as walking, fetch, or snuggling. Schedule time dedicated to providing play, walks, and relaxation. These activities not only provide a needed respite but support the bond between the handler and the service dog.

Attending class. Once the schedule is made, students will need to consider the classroom arrangements, such as the type of seating available and if a larger service animal can fit under a desk or table. Students will need to determine the optimal location for the service animal in the classroom (e.g., an aisle seat away from the door to avoid distractions). The student may also need to determine the best path to navigate through the classroom to help address issues such as other students' reactions to the animal, both positive and negative. Although service animals have legal access to the classroom and fear of dogs and allergies are not a reason to remove the animal, students may need to address the social landscape within the classroom.

Preparing for reactions. Some faculty and students will not be familiar with interacting with service animals. They may ask questions and attempt to interact with the animal. Additionally, transition time between classes may be impacted. Students who use service dogs on campuses are often stopped because people ask about their dog or want to interact with the dog. Students also need time to allow the dog to relieve. As a result, they periodically may be late for classes or meetings. Some service dogs are trained to relieve on command, and this handling skill can be helpful in maintaining time schedules.

Acceptance of the service dog and its legitimacy may also be an issue. Students with invisible disabilities have reported being questioned if they actually need the service dog's assistance and if the dog meets service dog status. Incidents of bullying have been reported as well. These issues are not unique to the college setting but may need to be addressed within this specific environment and through channels offered by the college (Hagelgans, 2016). Developing self-advocacy skills in advance (see chapter 11) can help the student prepare for confrontations. Proactively identifying resources and support systems on campus and contacting these sources before a problem arises can also be helpful.

SUMMARY

Transitioning from high school to another environment with a service animal is a complex process. Factors related to the demands of the new employment or educational environment, the impact of the disability, and the service animal must be considered. Examine the current and anticipated work or college environment to identify existing skills, needed skills, and unique challenges, including the impact of a disability. Expand the environmental analysis beyond the obvious environments and consider the specific context. Transition to employment, postsecondary education, and housing offer unique situations. Concerns such as transportation, access to the workplace and classrooms, and social issues should be considered. Legal knowledge regarding service animal law and self-advocacy skills are essential as well. Last, consider the well-being of the service animal in the next environment. Also, examine the handler's needs. Consider the impact of the disability and how the service animal mitigates it. Identify current and new tasks required in the next environment to promote access and success. Last, plan for the service animal's safety and well-being. Identify hazards and potential stressors and schedule rest breaks. Finally, ensure the service animal is living and working in a comfortable environment.

Overall, transition planning is an individualized process. Each transition will be unique given the distinctive dynamic between a service animal and handler and the nature of the environment. Transition involves considering the needs of beings, human or animal, at both ends of the leash.

CHAPTER 13

SUMMARY, IMPLICATIONS, AND A LOOK FORWARD

Children and dogs are as necessary to the welfare of the country as Wall Street and the railroads.

—Harry S. Truman

ADVANCED ORGANIZER

After reading this chapter, you will be able to:

- understand and apply the legal, educational, and access considerations involving service dogs in schools;
- recognize major issues involved in service dog use in general and in the school setting in particular and generate means for addressing these issues;
- identify the knowledge and skills educational professionals, families, and service dog handlers must possess to effectively use and accommodate a service animal in a school setting; and
- realize how strategic handling and practical problem-solving skills contribute to effective service animal use in schools.

THE USE OF SERVICE ANIMALS in schools is increasing. The functions service animals perform are diversifying as well. At the same time, the use of other assistance animals, such as therapy and emotional support animals, is expanding. School personnel are faced with the task of deciphering if an animal is indeed a service animal, making it difficult to determine legal coverage and access issues. The purpose of this book is to provide the most up-to-date and relevant guidance related to working with service animals in schools. We believe that *Service Animals in Schools: A Comprehensive Guide for Administrators, Teachers, Parents, and Students* serves this purpose and is a timely addition to service animal literature.

As we approach the tail end of this book, our goal is to summarize and apply the major legal, educational, access, and strategic handling issues discussed. We presented the case of Jonas and Jinx when discussing service dogs access in schools (see chapter 6). In the following section is an expanded version of this case to guide our discussion and summary of the legal, educational, access, and strategic handling (LEASH) elements.

Jonas and Jinx

Jonas Scepter is a second-grade boy with autism who is eligible for special education and related services. He recently transferred to a new school. The multidisciplinary team received a copy of his IEP from his previous school stating he can bring his service dog, Jinx, to school.

Jinx is a two-year-old golden retriever that recently completed service dog training. Jinx performs several tasks for Jonas. Jinx calms Jonas down when he becomes agitated by leaning against Jonas, interrupting Jonas's unwanted behaviors by nudging him, blocking Jonas if he attempts elopement behaviors such as running out of the classroom or schools, finding a designated person (e.g., teacher or mother) by running toward the person and barking to alert them that Jonas needs help, and providing overall comfort to Jonas by being present for him to pet.

During the first few visits, Jinx was unruly in the classroom. He barked excessively, startling students and interrupting instruction. Jinx pulled away from Jonas on several occasions and ran from the classroom into the hall. Jinx also ate a part of another student's lunch while in the cafeteria.

Due to these disruptive behaviors, the principal asks Jonas's mother to keep Jinx at home because he is out of control, and Jonas cannot take actions to regain control. The principal requests Jonas demonstrate Jinx's designated tasks to the multidisciplinary team prior to Jinx returning to school. Jonas's mother refuses, indicating the school is violating ADA by not allowing Jonas to bring Jinx in school because a provision for using a service dog is in Jonas's IEP. She is planning to file a due process lawsuit against the district.

Questions to consider:
- What legislation applies?
- What is the next step the district should take?
- What are the legal, educational, and access issues involved in this case?
- How could strategic handling impact the outcome?
- Can Jinx return to school? Why or why not?

LESSONS LEARNED FROM THIS CASE: SUMMARY AND IMPLICATIONS

Legal, Educational, and Access Issues

We sincerely wish that every service animal, when placed with a student in school, provides the necessary support for the student, and there are no problems with the animal. However, that is not the case. Just like not every paraprofessional or aide assigned to a student will help with resolving all the problems that might occur or providing a piece or form of technology will also not potentially solve the problems a student has, providing a service animal may or may not be the assistance the student needs. As will be noted throughout the chapter, it is the school district's obligation to ensure the student is provided a free appropriate public education. Service animals may help the student. They may not. But regardless of what tasks the service animal performs for the student, the school district still has to ensure the student makes progress and the goals and objectives delineated in the IEP are addressed.

Therefore, we are specifically recommending that districts continue to take data on the performance of the student and not just rely on the service animal for all (or even some) of the tasks. If a service animal is provided for prompting or redirection, does the student still need promoting or redirection after the service animal has started working in the school with the student? Does the student do better (defined based on the skills necessary) when the service animal is present? Or has the behavior of the student plateaued or even become worse? One can only make this determination with the use of regular and consistent data on the behaviors of the student.

Important Legal, Access, and Educational Considerations

The following section contains several important points to ponder when addressing legal, educational, and access issues for a student with a disability using a service animal in school.

Not all dogs are service dogs. Neither the IDEA nor Section 504 specifically address whether students with disabilities have the right to be accompanied by service animals on school grounds. However, the 2010 amendments to the Title II regulations implementing the ADA clarify some of the requirements for service animals.

As we have covered in other parts of this book, the 2010 Title II regulations of the Americans with Disabilities Act define "service animal" to mean:

> Any dog that is individually trained to do work or perform tasks for the benefit of an individual with a disability, including a physical, sensory, psychiatric, intellectual, or other mental disability. Other species of animals, whether wild or domestic, trained or untrained, are not service animals for the purposes of this definition. The work or tasks performed by a service animal must be directly related to the handler's disability. Examples of work or tasks include, but are not limited to, assisting individuals who are blind or have low vision with navigation and other tasks, alerting individuals who are deaf or hard of

hearing to the presence of people or sounds, providing nonviolent protection or rescue work, pulling a wheelchair, assisting an individual during a seizure, alerting individuals to the presence of allergens, retrieving items such as medicine or the telephone, providing physical support and assistance with balance and stability to individuals with mobility disabilities, and helping persons with psychiatric and neurological disabilities by preventing or interrupting impulsive or destructive behaviors.

Based on the specifics related to our case, when a student's dog is specially trained to prevent the child from shrieking, throwing tantrums, and eloping, it meets the definition of a service animal. But just providing nurture or support does not meet the need of a service animal. This is covered in other chapters where we highlight the differences between service animals and emotional support animals.

According to the Department of Justice, the distinction between a service animal and an emotional support animal turns on the work or tasks the animal performs and the specific training it received. While emotional support animals provide comfort or companionship simply by their presence, psychiatric service animals may perform tasks such as reminding an individual with a disability to take medication, performing safety checks or room searches for individuals with PTSD, interrupting self-mutilation, and removing disoriented individuals from dangerous situations (*Federal Register*, volume 75, p. 56195 [September 15, 2010]).

Section 504 and service animals. Section 504, which offers the same protections afforded by the ADA, applies to entities that receive federal funds, including public and charter schools (34 CFR 104.3 (f)). Schools need to modify their policies to allow for service animals, unless the animal is out of control or not housebroken.

Handlers. A service animal must be under the control of its handler. The service animal must have a harness, leash, or other tether, unless:

- the handler is unable, because of a disability, to use a harness, leash, or other tether; or
- the use of a harness, leash, or other tether would interfere with the service animal's safe, effective performance of work or tasks. In this case, the handler must use voice control, signals, or other effective means to control the service animal.

Service animals and free appropriate education. Title II and III of the ADA explain behavioral standards regarding service dog use, access rights by service dog handlers, and, in our case, access to schools. The ADA is very specific that service animals have access to areas the public can go, and this includes schools. However, and this is important, the service animal must be under the control of the handler at all times. This control can be by leash, harness, or tether. There may be instances where the disability of the handler prevents the use of a leash. In those instances, the service animal must be under control through either voice or signals. Additionally, and this is important for schools, the service animal must be housebroken. This means the service animal must be able to control, absent illness, waste elimination.

These are the standards that are expected of service animals when they are in schools. If the service animal is not under the control of the handler or there are problems with waste elimination, then the school can ask for the service animal to leave. What is important is that the child's access to the school must be maintained, and the educational program offered to the child must be made available. We will cover this more in a later section; however, the school must still provide a free appropriate public education to the child regardless of whether the service animal is available.

Questions the school may ask. As we have noted repeatedly throughout this book, not all animals are service animals. If it is not clear or immediately apparent that the animal is a service animal, there are two questions that the school can ask. First, the school may ask if the animal is a service animal. Second, the school may ask what task the dog is trained to perform. There are other logistical questions that may be asked, such as when is the service animal going to be provided access to the outdoors to relieve themselves, along with access to water during the day. Finally, service animals are not required to wear a vest, though many commonly do.

Specifically, schools cannot require a service animal to demonstrate the specific tasks as was requested in the Jonas and Jinx case, nor can the school ask about the nature of the student's disability. If you have a child who has arrived at school with a service animal and the district did not know there was a disability, there may be an issue related to Child Find, a component of IDEA requiring schools to identify, locate, and evaluate all children with disabilities. Therefore, if a child brings a service animal to school and the child is not eligible for special education and related services or eligible under Section 504 of the Rehabilitation Act, then the district should immediately complete a full evaluation of the child to ensure the identification of necessary services to assist the child in making progress in the curriculum.

Responsibility for the service animal. School districts are not responsible for the care or supervision of a service animal according to Title II of the ADA

(28 CFR 35.136 (e)). Schools may assist students with disabilities while they care for and supervise the service animals. This statement seemingly makes the situation unclear; however, schools need to provide accommodations to the student who uses a service animal similarly to how they provide accommodations to all students who have disabilities. However, the difference is the school district only needs to provide accommodations to the student. It does not have to provide care for the animal. An example of an accommodation could be to assist the student in taking the service animal outside so the animal could relieve itself. This accommodation is to the student but does not provide direct care for the animal because that is not the district's obligation.

Various courts have interpreted that when the animal is outside of the responsibility of the student, be it no longer tethered to the student or out of verbal command reach, the individuals who have the service animal are the ones providing care and supervision at that point. This is something school districts do not have to do. It is the responsibility of the handler to have care and responsibility for the service animal.

Additionally, it is not the responsibility of the district to be, or to provide, a handler for the service animal. It is, however, the responsibility of the district to ensure the student receives a free appropriate public education and the student makes progress on their IEP goals and objectives. As we have noted in multiple places throughout this book, the needs of the student drive the IEP goals, and the district needs to ensure the resources are available and provided for the student to receive those appropriate services.

Addressing Problems

Alternate services. As we have noted before, it is the school district's responsibility to ensure the student who receives special education is provided with a free appropriate public education. In the instances that a service animal is a part of the provision of services to the student, the IEP needs to have a back-up plan in case the service dog is not able to accompany the student and provide services due to illness, injury, or retirement or in case the service animal is asked to leave because it is having problems and the student (or handler) is not able to control the dog. In these instances, it is imperative that the IEP team meet to specifically identify the needs that were addressed by the service animal and develop a plan to address those needs without the service animal. A district cannot rely solely on the service animal; they have an obligation to provide services when the service dog is not present. It is actually good practice to develop the specifics of the plan that would be put into place before there is an incident with the service animal or it is not able to accompany the student. Therefore, hold the IEP team meeting prior to any incident and make sure that *all* of the student's needs are being fully addressed by the district, whether the service dog is present or not.

This IEP meeting should be like any other IEP team meeting, with all the necessary participants present, especially the parents. Work to address the specifics of the student's needs, and if a service dog is going to be used, maybe not all of the services the district would be expected to provide are necessary because of the service dog. However, as noted above, the district should be ready to step in the moment the service dog either is unavailable or causes problems preventing its attendance.

Just a reminder, the legal obligation of school districts is to provide an appropriate education, not the best one. The best education or the best level of services is a superlative race that would never be won.

Monitoring performance. As mentioned above, the district should also take data on the needs of the child and whether the service dog addresses those needs. Yes, the service animal will be present and will be there to assist the student with their specific needs, but the district cannot assume that just because the student has a service animal their needs are being addressed. Take regular observational data on the specific needs the student has and make a determination about whether the student still has unmet needs. If unmet needs exist, it is the obligation of the school district to develop a plan to address those needs and not just assume the service animal is doing its job. This is the same plan that should be used when we assign a one-on-one aide to a student or provide the student some technology to help with their needs. Take data, analyze the data, and make changes if necessary.

Litigation and legislation. We wish that there was not a need for litigation, everyone got along, and there were no disputes. However, there are often disagreements about services for students using a service animal. Disputes arise in response to the efforts of school personnel to provide accommodations that are disagreeable to parents or other parties or as a result of school personnel being perceived as unresponsive to the needs of the student. Bateman and Cline (2019) list conditions under which school districts are likely to experience due process complaints:

1. not complying with procedural requirements (e.g., insufficient notice of intent to change placement, denial of an IEP);
2. not providing appropriate services based on cost considerations (i.e., telling parents a particular service is appropriate but not providing it because it costs too much);

3. not providing appropriate education as a result of acquiescing to parental demands (i.e., the right to an education belongs to the child, not the parents); and
4. not acting promptly in providing services (e.g., waiting too long, not taking action in a reasonable time frame).

The litigation process in special education is called a due process hearing. A due process hearing (often referred to just as due process) is a formal presentation of facts so that a due process hearing officer, as an impartial third party, can hear both sides of a dispute, examine the issues, and render a decision to resolve the issues. The purpose of a due process hearing is to resolve a dispute over the identification, evaluation, or educational placement of or related to the provision of a free appropriate public education (FAPE) to students with, or thought to be, eligible for special education and related services.

A due process hearing is the appropriate venue for disputes related to a child's education and whether the student is making progress in the curriculum. Service animals do not, however, neatly fit in the role of ensuring a student is making progress in their curriculum. There may be issues of whether the service animal has access to the educational environment, or the parents feel the student is being discriminated against because of the need or use of a service animal. In these instances the appropriate venue for resolving the dispute or pursuing litigation may be under the Americans with Disabilities Act or Section 504. The recent Supreme Court case *Fry v. Napoleon* (2017) clarified that when a parent is seeking a remedy that cannot be delivered by a due process hearing, then they can pursue litigation in other courts. However, it is clear that if a parent is seeking restitution or remedies relating to the educational service of their student with a disability, a due process hearing is the appropriate venue.

Strategic Handling

Legal, educational, and access considerations provide a parameter for service dog use in school. They determine the rights afforded to a service animal and its ability to meet the student's needs. Strategic handling involves the interaction between the handler, animal, and environment. It impacts the day-to-day use of the service animal and the ultimate success of the team.

Service animals must be fully trained to perform their designated task and be capable of performing them in the school environment. However, things do not always go as planned. In the following section, implications for strategic handling are discussed.

Asking for help. Not every handler who acquires a service animal has knowledge of animal training, and not every animal is ready to work in the school environment. If mistakes happen, acknowledge them, address them, and seek assistance if needed. Assistance may take the form of assisting the handler, retraining the dog to perform designated tasks, or supporting the dog with environmental distraction.

In the case of Jonas and Jinx, at first glance, the service dog, Jinx, is making errors and appears to be out of control. Handler, dog, and environmental factors exist within this case. Note that Jonas is a second grader who may have limited dog handling experience. Also notice that some of Jinx's behavior may be misplaced attempts at performing a designated task of alerting (i.e., barking) and finding help (running from Jonas to a designated person), triggered through lack of training or a miscue from Jonas. Jinx also demonstrates an inability to deal with environmental distractions like the presence of accessible food. This team requires assistance to determine the source of the errors and remediate them. There are times when it is best to remove a service animal from a situation until either the handler is able to control it or the animal performs tasks reliably and is capable of handling the distractions of a school situation. A trainer may be brought in to help the handler and service animal in the school environment if needed.

Define control. Control is contextual. Service animal behaviors may be perceived as appropriate by one party involved and inappropriate to another. Jonas's parents may perceive Jinx's running away and barking as useful while school personnel view it as unruly. The family, the handler, and the school need to agree on what controlled behavior looks like within the school setting.

Advocate and inform. A student using a service animal and their family may need to advocate for the service animal. The general public is often misinformed about service animal laws and rights. They may impede access or inappropriately interact with the service animal. Expect that school personnel, teachers, and students will need training on service animal law and etiquette. Likewise, students using service animals should know their rights and be prepared to advocate when the access rights or legitimacy of the service animal is questioned. They should also be prepared to handle unwanted attention and interruptions. Directly practice handling these situations in advance and be ready to use them.

Collaborate and communicate. Service animal issues do not always revolve around the behavior of the animal and handler. Issues can arise from the presence of the animal within the school setting. Some students or school personnel may be afraid of or allergic to the service animal. These are not reasons to exclude a service animal from a school. IDEA and Section 504 dictate the access and educational rights of the service animal, but they do not prevent compromise. A student using a service animal is part of the classroom and school community. The use of a service animal is only one aspect of their being. They may be willing to compromise and help work out solutions if they are invited to be part of the discussion. Consider bringing parties together to explore solutions to situations and allowing a compromise to happen before removing or restricting a service animal. Many handlers are glad to compromise and show consideration.

Remember the other end of the leash. Service animals can provide vital support to students with disabilities. However, they can only provide this support when they are cared for and treated properly. Service animals are one of the few living accommodations provided to students with disabilities. They must be treated with respect, and their needs must be met.

SUMMARY

As we have reached the end of our LEASH, let us reflect on Harry S. Truman's quote: "Children and dogs are as necessary to the welfare of the country as Wall Street and the railroads." Service animals can be a means for providing vital support to students with disabilities in schools and beyond. Service animal use must be carefully considered; time, effort, and skill are involved. Service animal use should result in meaningful outcomes for students with disabilities. An understanding of the legal, educational, and access rights provides the opportunity for students with disabilities to use service animals in schools. Strategic handling supports the actualization of the benefits derived from service animal use.

APPENDIX 1

DOJ AND SERVICE ANIMALS

U.S. Department of Justice
Civil Rights Division
Disability Rights Section

Frequently Asked Questions about Service Animals and the ADA

Many people with disabilities use a service animal in order to fully participate in everyday life. Dogs can be trained to perform many important tasks to assist people with disabilities, such as providing stability for a person who has difficulty walking, picking up items for a person who uses a wheelchair, preventing a child with autism from wandering away, or alerting a person who has hearing loss when someone is approaching from behind.

The Department of Justice continues to receive many questions about how the Americans with Disabilities Act (ADA) applies to service animals. The ADA requires State and local government agencies, businesses, and non-profit organizations (covered entities) that provide goods or services to the public to make "reasonable modifications" in their policies, practices, or procedures when necessary to accommodate people with disabilities. The service animal rules fall under this general principle. Accordingly, entities that have a "no pets" policy generally must modify the policy to allow service animals into their facilities. This publication provides guidance on the ADA's service animal provisions and should be read in conjunction with the publication.

DEFINITION OF A SERVICE ANIMAL

Q1. **What is a service animal?**

A. Under the ADA, a service animal is defined as a dog that has been individually trained to do work or perform tasks for an individual with a disability. The task(s) performed by the dog must be directly related to the person's disability.

Q2. What does "do work or perform tasks" mean?

A. The dog must be trained to take a specific action when needed to assist the person with a disability. For example, a person with diabetes may have a dog that is trained to alert him when his blood sugar reaches high or low levels. A person with depression may have a dog that is trained to remind her to take her medication. Or, a person who has epilepsy may have a dog that is trained to detect the onset of a seizure and then help the person remain safe during the seizure.

Q3. Are emotional support, therapy, comfort, or companion animals considered service animals under the ADA?

A. No. These terms are used to describe animals that provide comfort just by being with a person. Because they have *not* been trained to perform a specific job or task, they do *not* qualify as service animals under the ADA. However, some State or local governments have laws that allow people to take emotional support animals into public places. You may check with your State and local government agencies to find out about these laws.

Q4. If someone's dog calms them when having an anxiety attack, does this qualify it as a service animal?

A. It depends. The ADA makes a distinction between psychiatric service animals and emotional support animals. If the dog has been trained to sense that an anxiety attack is about to happen and take a specific action to help avoid the attack or lessen its impact, that would qualify as a service animal. However, if the dog's mere presence provides comfort, that would not be considered a service animal under the ADA.

Q5. Does the ADA require service animals to be professionally trained?

A. No. People with disabilities have the right to train the dog themselves and are not required to use a professional service dog training program.

Q6. Are service-animals-in-training considered service animals under the ADA?

A. No. Under the ADA, the dog must already be trained before it can be taken into public places. However, some State or local laws cover animals that are still in training.

GENERAL RULES

Q7. **What questions can a covered entity's employees ask to determine if a dog is a service animal?**

A. In situations where it is not obvious that the dog is a service animal, staff may ask only two specific questions: (1) is the dog a service animal required because of a disability? and (2) what work or task has the dog been trained to perform? Staff are not allowed to request any documentation for the dog, require that the dog demonstrate its task, or inquire about the nature of the person's disability.

Q8. **Do service animals have to wear a vest or patch or special harness identifying them as service animals?**

A. No. The ADA does not require service animals to wear a vest, ID tag, or specific harness.

Q9. **Who is responsible for the care and supervision of a service animal?**

A. The handler is responsible for caring for and supervising the service animal, which includes toileting, feeding, and grooming and veterinary care. Covered entities are not obligated to supervise or otherwise care for a service animal.

Q10. **Can a person bring a service animal with them as they go through a salad bar or other self-service food lines?**

A. Yes. Service animals must be allowed to accompany their handlers to and through self-service food lines. Similarly, service animals may not be prohibited from communal food preparation areas, such as are commonly found in shelters or dormitories.

Q11. **Can hotels assign designated rooms for guests with service animals, out of consideration for other guests?**

A. No. A guest with a disability who uses a service animal must be provided the same opportunity to reserve any available room at the hotel as other guests without disabilities. They may not be restricted to "pet-friendly" rooms.

Q12. **Can hotels charge a cleaning fee for guests who have service animals?**

A. No. Hotels are not permitted to charge guests for cleaning the hair or dander shed by a service animal. However, if a guest's service animal causes damages to a guest room, a hotel is permitted to charge the same fee for damages as charged to other guests.

Q13. Can people bring more than one service animal into a public place?

A. Generally, yes. Some people with disabilities may use more than one service animal to perform different tasks. For example, a person who has a visual disability and a seizure disorder may use one service animal to assist with way-finding and another that is trained as a seizure alert dog. Other people may need two service animals for the same task, such as a person who needs two dogs to assist him or her with stability when walking. Staff may ask the two permissible questions (See Question 7) about each of the dogs. If both dogs can be accommodated, both should be allowed in. In some circumstances, however, it may not be possible to accommodate more than one service animal. For example, in a crowded small restaurant, only one dog may be able to fit under the table. The only other place for the second dog would be in the aisle, which would block the space between tables. In this case, staff may request that one of the dogs be left outside.

Q14. Does a hospital have to allow an in-patient with a disability to keep a service animal in his or her room?

A. Generally, yes. Service animals must be allowed in patient rooms and anywhere else in the hospital the public and patients are allowed to go. They cannot be excluded on the grounds that staff can provide the same services.

Q15. What happens if a patient who uses a service animal is admitted to the hospital and is unable to care for or supervise their animal?

A. If the patient is not able to care for the service animal, the patient can make arrangements for a family member or friend to come to the hospital to provide these services, as it is always preferable that the service animal and its handler not be separated, or to keep the dog during the hospitalization. If the patient is unable to care for the dog and is unable to arrange for someone else to care for the dog, the hospital may place the dog in a boarding facility until the patient is released, or make other appropriate arrangements. However, the hospital must give the patient the opportunity to make arrangements for the dog's care before taking such steps.

Q16. Must a service animal be allowed to ride in an ambulance with its handler?

A. Generally, yes. However, if the space in the ambulance is crowded and the dog's presence would interfere with the emergency medical staff's ability to treat the patient, staff should make other arrangements to have the dog transported to the hospital.

CERTIFICATION AND REGISTRATION

Q17. Does the ADA require that service animals be certified as service animals?

A. No. Covered entities may not require documentation, such as proof that the animal has been certified, trained, or licensed as a service animal, as a condition for entry.

There are individuals and organizations that sell service animal certification or registration documents online. These documents do not convey any rights under the ADA and the Department of Justice does not recognize them as proof that the dog is a service animal.

Q18. My city requires all dogs to be vaccinated. Does this apply to my service animal?

A. Yes. Individuals who have service animals are not exempt from local animal control or public health requirements.

Q19. My city requires all dogs to be registered and licensed. Does this apply to my service animal?

A. Yes. Service animals are subject to local dog licensing and registration requirements.

Q20. My city requires me to register my dog as a service animal. Is this legal under the ADA?

A. No. Mandatory registration of service animals is not permissible under the ADA. However, as stated above, service animals are subject to the same licensing and vaccination rules that are applied to all dogs.

Q21. My city / college offers a voluntary registry program for people with disabilities who use service animals and provides a special tag identifying the dogs as service animals. Is this legal under the ADA?

A. Yes. Colleges and other entities, such as local governments, may offer voluntary registries. Many communities maintain a voluntary registry that serves a public purpose, for example, to ensure that emergency staff know to look for service animals during an emergency evacuation process. Some offer a benefit, such as a reduced dog license fee, for individuals who register their service animals. Registries for purposes like this are permitted under the ADA. An entity may not, however, require that a dog be registered as a service animal as a condition of being permitted in public places. This would be a violation of the ADA.

BREEDS

Q22. Can service animals be any breed of dog?

A. Yes. The ADA does not restrict the type of dog breeds that can be service animals.

Q23. Can individuals with disabilities be refused access to a facility based solely on the breed of their service animal?

A. No. A service animal may not be excluded based on assumptions or stereotypes about the animal's breed or how the animal might behave. However, if a particular service animal behaves in a way that poses a direct threat to the health or safety of others, has a history of such behavior, or is not under the control of the handler, that animal may be excluded. If an animal is excluded for such reasons, staff must still offer their goods or services to the person without the animal present.

Q24. If a municipality has an ordinance that bans certain dog breeds, does the ban apply to service animals?

A. No. Municipalities that prohibit specific breeds of dogs must make an exception for a service animal of a prohibited breed, unless the dog poses a direct threat to the health or safety of others. Under the "direct threat" provisions of the ADA, local jurisdictions need to determine, on a case-by-case basis, whether a particular service animal can be excluded based on that particular animal's actual behavior or history, but they may not exclude a service animal because of fears or generalizations about how an animal or breed might behave. It is important to note that breed restrictions differ significantly from jurisdiction to jurisdiction. In fact, some jurisdictions have no breed restrictions.

EXCLUSION OF SERVICE ANIMALS

Q25. When can service animals be excluded?

A. The ADA does not require covered entities to modify policies, practices, or procedures if it would "fundamentally alter" the nature of the goods, services, programs, or activities provided to the public. Nor does it overrule legitimate safety requirements. If admitting service animals would fundamentally alter the nature of a service or program, service animals may be prohibited. In addition, if a particular service animal is out of control and the handler does not take effective action to control it, or if it is not housebroken, that animal may be excluded.

Q26. When might a service dog's presence fundamentally alter the nature of a service or program provided to the public?

A. In most settings, the presence of a service animal will not result in a fundamental alteration. However, there are some exceptions. For example, at a boarding school, service animals could be restricted from a specific area of a dormitory reserved specifically for students with allergies to dog dander. At a zoo, service animals can be restricted from areas where the animals on display are the natural prey or natural predators of dogs, where the presence of a dog would be disruptive, causing the displayed animals to behave aggressively or become agitated. They cannot be restricted from other areas of the zoo.

Q27. What does under control mean? Do service animals have to be on a leash? Do they have to be quiet and not bark?

A. The ADA requires that service animals be under the control of the handler at all times. In most instances, the handler will be the individual with a disability or a third party who accompanies the individual with a disability. In the school (K–12) context and in similar settings, the school or similar entity may need to provide some assistance to enable a particular student to handle his or her service animal. The service animal must be harnessed, leashed, or tethered while in public places unless these devices interfere with the service animal's work or the person's disability prevents use of these devices. In that case, the person must use voice, signal, or other effective means to maintain control of the animal. For example, a person who uses a wheelchair may use a long, retractable leash to allow her service animal to pick up or retrieve items. She may not allow the dog to wander away from her and must maintain control of the dog, even if it is retrieving an item at a distance from her. Or, a returning veteran who has PTSD and has great difficulty entering unfamiliar spaces may have a dog that is trained to enter a space, check to see that no threats are there, and come back and signal that it is safe to enter. The dog must be off leash to do its job, but may be leashed at other times. Under control also means that a service animal should not be allowed to bark repeatedly in a lecture hall, theater, library, or other quiet place. However, if a dog barks just once, or barks because someone has provoked it, this would not mean that the dog is out of control.

Q28. What can my staff do when a service animal is being disruptive?

A. If a service animal is out of control and the handler does not take effective action to control it, staff may request that the animal be removed from the premises.

Q29. Are hotel guests allowed to leave their service animals in their hotel room when they leave the hotel?

A. No, the dog must be under the handler's control at all times.

Q30. What happens if a person thinks a covered entity's staff has discriminated against him or her?

A. Individuals who believe that they have been illegally denied access or service because they use service animals may file a complaint with the U.S. Department of Justice. Individuals also have the right to file a private lawsuit in Federal court charging the entity with discrimination under the ADA.

MISCELLANEOUS

Q31. Are stores required to allow service animals to be placed in a shopping cart?

A. Generally, the dog must stay on the floor, or the person must carry the dog. For example, if a person with diabetes has a glucose alert dog, he may carry the dog in a chest pack so it can be close to his face to allow the dog to smell his breath to alert him of a change in glucose levels.

Q32. Are restaurants, bars, and other places that serve food or drink required to allow service animals to be seated on chairs or allow the animal to be fed at the table?

A. No. Seating, food, and drink are provided for customer use only. The ADA gives a person with a disability the right to be accompanied by his or her service animal, but covered entities are not required to allow an animal to sit or be fed at the table.

Q33. Are gyms, fitness centers, hotels, or municipalities that have swimming pools required to allow a service animal in the pool with its handler?

A. No. The ADA does not override public health rules that prohibit dogs in swimming pools. However, service animals must be allowed on the pool deck and in other areas where the public is allowed to go.

Q34. Are churches, temples, synagogues, mosques, and other places of worship required to allow individuals to bring their service animals into the facility?

A. No. Religious institutions and organizations are specifically exempt from the ADA. However, there may be State laws that apply to religious organizations.

Q35. Do apartments, mobile home parks, and other residential properties have to comply with the ADA?

A. The ADA applies to housing programs administered by State and local governments, such as public housing authorities, and by places of public accommodation, such as public and private universities. In addition, the Fair Housing Act applies to virtually all types of housing, both public and privately-owned, including housing covered by the ADA. Under the Fair Housing Act, housing providers are obligated to permit, as a reasonable accommodation, the use of animals that work, provide assistance, or perform tasks that benefit persons with disabilities, or provide emotional support to alleviate a symptom or effect of a disability. For information about these Fair Housing Act requirements see HUD's Notice on

APPENDIX 1

Service Animals and Assistance Animals for People with Disabilities in Housing and HUD-funded Programs.

Q36. Do Federal agencies, such as the U.S. Department of Veterans Affairs, have to comply with the ADA?

A. No. Section 504 of the Rehabilitation Act of 1973 is the Federal law that protects the rights of people with disabilities to participate in Federal programs and services. For information or to file a complaint, contact the agency's equal opportunity office.

Q37. Do commercial airlines have to comply with the ADA?

A. No. The Air Carrier Access Act is the Federal law that protects the rights of people with disabilities in air travel. For information or to file a complaint, contact the U.S. Department of Transportation, Aviation Consumer Protection Division, at 202-366-2220.

RESOURCES

For more information about the ADA, please visit our website or call our toll-free number.

ADA WEBSITE

www.ADA.gov
To receive e-mail notifications when new ADA information is available, visit the ADA Website's home page and click the link near the bottom of the right-hand column.

ADA INFORMATION LINE

800-514-0301 (Voice) and 800-514-0383 (TTY)
M–W, F 9:30 a.m.–5:30 p.m., Th 12:30 p.m.–5:30 p.m. (Eastern Time) to speak with an ADA Specialist. Calls are confidential.

The Americans with Disabilities Act authorizes the Department of Justice (the Department) to provide technical assistance to individuals and entities that have rights or responsibilities under the Act. This document provides informal guidance to assist you in understanding the ADA and the Department's regulations.

This guidance document is not intended to be a final agency action, has no legally binding effect, and may be rescinded or modified in the Department's complete discretion, in accordance with applicable laws. The Department's guidance documents, including this guidance, do not establish legally enforceable responsibilities beyond what is required by the terms of the applicable statutes, regulations, or binding judicial precedent.

For people with disabilities, this publication is available in alternate formats.
Duplication of this document is encouraged.
July 2015

APPENDIX 2

SAMPLE SCHOOL POLICY

SCHOOL DISTRICT NAME

SERVICE ANIMALS IN SCHOOLS

I. PURPOSE

The purpose of this policy is to establish procedures for the use of service animals by students, employees, and visitors within school buildings and on school grounds.

II. DEFINITIONS

A. Service Animal

Service Animal means any dog (regardless of breed or size) or miniature horse that is individually trained to do work or perform "work or tasks" for the benefit of an individual with a disability, including a physical, sensory, psychiatric, intellectual, or other mental disability.

Service animals are working animals that perform valuable functions; they are not pets. Service animals do not include wild animals, farm animals, rodents, or animals whose sole function is to provide emotional support, comfort, therapy, companionship, therapeutic benefits, or to promote emotional well-being. Other species of animals, whether wild or domestic, trained or untrained, are not service animals for purposes of this definition.

B. Handler

A "handler" is an individual with a disability who is accompanied by a service animal or a trainer who is accompanied by a service animal. For purposes of this policy, the terms "handler" and "individual with a disability" may be used interchangeably.

C. **Work or Tasks**
1. Work or tasks are those tasks performed by a Service Animal. The "work or tasks" must be directly related to the handler's disability.
2. Examples of work or tasks include, but are not limited to:
   a. assisting individuals who are blind or have low vision with navigation and other tasks;
   b. alerting individuals who are deaf or hard of hearing to the presence of people or sounds;
   c. providing non-violent protection or rescue work;
   d. pulling a wheelchair;
   e. assisting an individual during a seizure;
   f. alerting individuals to the presence of allergens;
   g. retrieving items such as medicine or the telephone, providing physical support and assistance with balance and stability to individuals with mobility disabilities; and
   h. helping persons with psychiatric and neurological disabilities by preventing or interrupting impulsive or destructive behaviors.
3. The crime deterrent effects of an animal's presence and the provision of emotional support, well-being, comfort, or companionship do not constitute work or tasks for the purposes of this definition.

D. **Trainer**

A "trainer" is a person who is training a service animal and is affiliated with a recognized training program for service animals.

III. **ACCESS TO PROGRAMS AND ACTIVITIES; PERMITTED INQUIRIES**

A. Prior to bringing a service animal on district property, facilities, or vehicles, the parent/guardian of a student with a disability or the employee will be asked to meet with a planning team to prepare for effective integration of the service animal into the school environment. This meeting will allow for planning regarding schedules, transportation, student instructional day, and extracurricular activities, as well as a communication plan to the school community in preparation for the service animal. In addition, the parent/guardian or employee will be asked to review the Administrative Procedures and to complete the **Service Animal Registration/Agreement form** to verify their understanding of Administrative Procedures.

B. In general, handlers (i.e., individuals with disabilities) or trainers are permitted to be accompanied by their service animals in all areas of school district properties where members of the public, students, and employees are allowed to go. A handler has the right to be accompanied by a service animal whenever and to the same extent that the handler has the right

1. to be present on school district property or in school district facilities;
2. to attend or participate in a school sponsored event, activity, or program; or
3. to be transported in a vehicle that is operated by or on behalf of the school district.

C. When an individual with a disability brings a service animal to school district property, school district employees shall not ask about the nature or extent of a person's disability, but may make the following two inquiries to determine whether the animal qualifies as a service animal:

1. if the animal is required because of a disability; and
2. what work or tasks the animal has been trained to perform.

D. School district employees shall not make these inquiries of an individual with a disability bringing a service animal to school district property when it is readily apparent that an animal is trained to do work or perform tasks for an individual with a disability.

E. An individual with a disability may not be required to provide documentation such as proof that the animal has been certified, trained, or licensed as a service animal.

IV. REQUIREMENTS FOR ALL SERVICE ANIMALS

A. A service animal must be under the control of its handler.

B. The service animal must be individually trained to do work or tasks for the benefit of the individual with a disability.

C. A service animal must have a harness, leash, or another tether, unless either the handler is unable because of a disability to use a harness, leash, or another tether, or the use of a harness, leash, or other tether would interfere with the service animal's safe, effective performance of work or tasks, in which case the service animal must be otherwise under the handler's control (e.g., voice control, signals, or other effective means).

D. The service animal must be housebroken.

E. The service animal must be properly and currently vaccinated.

V. CARE OF, AND RESPONSIBILITY FOR, SERVICE ANIMALS; LIABILITY

A. The handler is solely responsible for the care and supervision of the service animal including, but not limited to, feeding, watering, cleaning, toileting, cleanup, and stain removal.

B. The district is not responsible for providing a staff member to walk the service animal or to provide any other care or assistance to the animal. Neither the school district nor its staff will assume such responsibilities. In the case of a young child or a student with disabilities who is unable to care for or supervise his or her service animal, the parent is responsible for providing care and supervision of the animal. Issues related to the care and supervision of service animals will be addressed on a case-by-case basis at the discretion of the building administrator.

C. Individuals with disabilities who are assisted by service animals are responsible for providing the supplies and equipment needed by the service animal.

D. Owners of service animals are liable for any harm or injury caused by the service animal to other students, staff, visitors, and/or property.

VI. REMOVAL OR EXCLUSION OF A SERVICE ANIMAL

A. A school official may require a handler to remove a service animal from school district property, a school building, or a school-sponsored program or activity, if:

1. the service animal is out of control and the handler does not take effective action to control it;
2. the service animal is not housebroken;
3. the presence of the animal would fundamentally alter the nature of a service, program, or activity;
4. the service animal poses a direct threat to the health and safety of others that cannot be eliminated by reasonable modifications; or
5. the handler fails to submit proof of current vaccinations and immunizations of the service animal.

B. If the service animal is properly excluded, the school district shall give the individual with a disability the opportunity to participate in the service, program, or activity without the service animal, unless such individual has violated a law or school rule or regulation that would warrant the removal of the individual.

VII. ADDITIONAL LIMITATIONS FOR MINIATURE HORSES

A. In assessing whether a miniature horse may be permitted in a school building or on school grounds as a service animal, the following factors shall be considered:

1. the type, size, and weight of the miniature horse and whether the facility can accommodate these features;
2. whether the handler has sufficient control of the miniature horse;
3. whether the miniature horse is housebroken;
4. whether the miniature horse's presence in a specific building or on school grounds compromises legitimate safety requirements that are necessary for safe operation; and
5. whether the miniature horse's presence is contrary to any other provision of this policy.

VIII. ALLERGIES; FEAR OF ANIMALS

If a student or employee notifies the school district he or she is allergic to a service animal, the school district will balance the rights of the individuals involved. In general, allergies that are not life-threatening are not a valid reason for prohibiting the presence of a service animal. Fear of animals is generally not a valid reason for prohibiting the presence of a service animal.

IX. ANIMALS FOR STUDENTS WITH INDIVIDUALIZED EDUCATION PROGRAMS/INDIVIDUAL FAMILY SERVICE PLANS OR SECTION 504 PLANS

If a student with an Individualized Education Program/Individual Family Service Plan or a student with a Section 504 plan seeks to bring an animal onto school property that is not a service animal, the request shall be referred to the student's IEP Team or Section 504 Team, as appropriate, to determine whether the animal is necessary for the student to receive a free appropriate public education ("FAPE").

X. SERVICE ANIMALS FOR EMPLOYEES

Use of a service animal by a school district employee who is a qualified individual with a disability will be allowed when such use is necessary to enable the employee to perform the essential functions of his or her position or to enjoy the benefits of employment in a manner comparable to those similarly situated non-disabled employees.

[District Name]
Service Animal Registration/Agreement

Owner: _____ Student: _____

Name of handler: _____

Type of service animal: _____

Documentation is attached to verify that the service animal is:

____ **Properly and currently vaccinated.**

____ **Covered by adequate liability insurance.**

I have read and understand the [District Name] Administrative Procedures related to Service Animals and will abide by the terms of the procedure.

I understand that if my service animal is: out of control and/or the animal's handler does not effectively control the animal's behavior; is not housebroken or the animal's presence or behavior fundamentally interferes with the functions of the School District; or poses a direct threat to the health and safety of others that cannot be eliminated by reasonable modifications; or the handler fails to submit proof of current vaccinations and immunizations of the service animal, the School District has the discretion to exclude or remove my service animal from its property.

I agree to be responsible for any and all damage to School District property, personal property, and any injuries to individuals caused by my service animal. I agree to indemnify, defend, and hold harmless [District Name] from and against any and all claims, actions, suits, judgments, and demands brought by any party arising on account of, or in connection with, any activity of or damage caused by my service animal.

_____   _____
Owner signature   Date

_____   _____
Administrator   Date

BIBLIOGRAPHY

ADA Coordinator Training Certification Program. (2018). *Service animals & the ADA: Quick guide for business owners*. ADA Now. http://www.adanowonline.org/winter 2018article1.html

ADA Network. (2021, November 11). *Service animal misconceptions*. https://adata.org/service-animal-resource-hub/misconceptions

American Kennel Club. (n.d.). *Canine Good Citizens Test*. https://www.akc.org/products-services/training-programs/canine-good-citizen/take-the-test/

Americans with Disabilities Act of 1990, 42 U.S.C. § 12101 et seq. (1990). https://www.ada.gov/pubs/adastatute08.htm

Americans with Disabilities Act of 1990, Pub. L. No. 101-336, § 2, 104 Stat. 328 (1991).

Bateman, D. F., & Cline, J. L. (2019). *Special education leadership: Building effective programming in schools*. New York: Routledge.

Batt, L. S., Batt, M. S., Baguley, J. A., & McGreevy, P. D. (2008). Factors associated with success in guide dog training, *Journal of Veterinary Behavior, 3*(8), 143–51.

Baughman, P., Foreman, A., Parenti, L., Scotti, J. R., Meade, B. J., Wilson, M. E., & Wirth, O. (2015, Summer). APDT Research Spotlight: Project ROVER's survey of assistance dog providers. *APDT Chronicle of the Dog*, 30–31.

Bauman, A., Owen, K. B., Torske, M. O., Ding, D., Krokstad, S., & Stamatakis, E. (2020). Does dog ownership really prolong survival? A revised meta-analysis and reappraisal of the evidence. *Circulation: Cardiovascular Quality and Outcomes, 13*(10). https://doi.org/10.1161/CIRCOUTCOMES.120.006907

Brooks, R. B. (2012, February 20). *Animals and the Salem witch trials*. History of Massachusetts. https://historyofmassachusetts.org/animals-in-the-salem-witch-trials/

Corson, S. A., Corson, E. O., Gwynne, P. H., & Arnold, L. E. (1977). Pet dogs as nonverbal communication links in hospital psychiatry. *Comprehensive Psychiatry, 18*(1), 61–72. http://dx.doi.org/10.1016/S0010-440X(77)80008-4

Duffy, D. L., & Serpell, J. A. (2012). Predictive validity of a method for evaluating temperament in young guide and service dogs. *Applied Animal Behaviour Science, 13*(1–2), 99–109.

Endrew F. v. Douglas County School District Re-1, 798, F.3d 1329 (10th Cir. 2015), vacated and remanded, 137 S.Ct. 988, 580 U.S. ___ (2017).

Ewoldt, K. B., Dieterich, C. A., & Brady, K. P. (2020). Service animals in preK–12 schools: Legal and policy implications for school leaders. *NASSP Bulletin, 104*(3), 220–34. https://doi.org/10.1177/0192636520923394

Franke, M. (2020, March 26). *Bonnie Bergin: The first service dog team*. Paws for Purple Hearts. https://pawsforpurplehearts.org/bonnie-bergin-the-first-service-dog-team/

Fry v. Napoleon et al., 580 U. S. ____ (2017).

Glenn, M. K., Foreman, A. M, Wierh, O., Shahan, K. M., Meade, B. J., & Torne, K. L. (2017). Legislation and other legal issues relevant in choosing to partner with a service dog in the workplace. *Journal of Rehabilitation, 83*(2), 17–26.

Grace, K. (2019). *Things service dogs in public should and should not do* [Blog post]. Anything Pawsable. https://anythingpawsable.com/things-service-dogs-public/

Greatbatch, I., Gosling, R. J., & Allen, S. (2015). Quantifying search dog effectiveness in a terrestrial search and rescue environment. *Wilderness & Environmental Medicine, 26*(3), 327–34. http://dx.doi.org/10.1016/j.wem.2015.02.009

Hagelgans, B. (2016, June 2). Bullied on campus for my invisible illness & service dog. *York Daily Record*. https://www.ydr.com/story/opinion/columnists/2016/06/02/bullied-campus-my-invisible-illness-service-dog-column/85208632/

Harmon, S., Street, M., Bateman, D. F., & Yell, M. P. (2020). Developing present levels of academic achievement and functional performance statements for IEPs. *Teaching Exceptional Children, 52*(5), 320–32.

Hildebrant, K. (2016). *Service dogs in the school setting*. Ohio State Bar Association. https://www.ohiobar.org/ForPublic/Resources/LawYouCanUse/Pages/LawYouCanUse-683.aspx

Individuals with Disabilities Education Act, 20 U.S.C. § 1400 (2004).

International Association of Assistance Dog Partners (n.d.). *IAADP minimum training standards for public access*. https://www.iaadp.org/iaadp-minimum-training-standards-for-public-access.html

Kalof, L. (2007). *Looking at animals in human history*. Chicago: University of Chicago Press.

Kassem, S. (2011). *Rise up and salute the sun: The writings of Suzy Kassem*. Boston: Awakened Press.

Kelch, T. G., (2013). A short history of (mostly) western animal law: Part II. *Animal Law Review, 19*, 347–90.

Kirk, R. G. (2014). In dogs we trust? Intersubjectivity, response-able relations, and the making of mine detector dogs. *Journal of the History of the Behavioral Sciences, 50*(1), 1–36. http://dx.doi.org/10.1002/jhbs.21642

Kruger, K. A., & Serpell, J. A. (2010). Animal-assisted interventions in mental health: Definitions and theoretical foundations. In A. H. Fine (Ed.), *Handbook on animal-assisted therapy: Theoretical foundations and guidelines for practice* (pp. 33–48). San Diego: Elsevier Academic Press. https://doi.org/10.1016/B978-0-12-381453-1.10003-0

Kuzma, C. (2018, November 16). Everything you need to know before getting a service dog. *Vice*. https://www.vice.com/en/article/j5zmak/everything-you-need-to-know-before-getting-a-service-dog

Lalliss, C. (2019, Oct 16). 5 things I've learned from having a service dog in college. *The Mighty*. https://themighty.com/2019/10/service-dog-college/https://themighty.com/2019/10/service-dog-college/

Levinson, B. M. (1962). The dog as a "co-therapist." *Mental Hygiene, 46*, 59–65.

MacNamara, M., Moga, J., & Pachel, C. (2015). What's love got to do with it? Selecting animals for animal-assisted mental health interventions. In A. Fine (Ed.), *Handbook on animal-assisted therapy* (4th ed., pp. 101–113). San Diego: Elsevier Academic Press.

Malamud, R. (2013). Service Animals: Serve us animals: Serve us, animals. *Social Alternatives, 32*(4), 34.

McDonald v. Department of Environmental Quality, 351 Mont. 243 (MONT. 2009).

Mills, M. (2017). Invisible disabilities, visible service dogs: The discrimination of service dog handlers. *Disability & Society, 32*(5), 635–56. https://doi.org/10.1080/09687599.2017.1307718

Moldin, S. J. (2008). *Transition to adulthood: The experience of youth with physical disabilities living with a service dog*. PhD dissertation, Indiana University, Bloomington, Indiana.

Monovisions. (2018, February 22). Vintage: Trench rats killed by terriers during World War I. https://monovisions.com/vintage-trench-rats-killed-by-terriers-during-world-war-i/

Morris, V. (2015). *Responsible service dog handling*. Psychiatric Service Dog Partners. https://www.psychdogpartners.org/wp-content/uploads/2015/08/Responsible-Service-Dog-Handling.pdf

Nahm, N., Lubin, J., Lubin, J., Bankwitz, B. K., Castelaz, M., Chen, X., ... & Totten, V. Y. (2012). Therapy dogs in the emergency department. *Western Journal of Emergency Medicine, 13*(4), 363–65. https://doi.org/10.5811/westjem.2011.5.6574

Nieforth, L. O., Rodriguez, K. E., & O'Haire, M. E. (2021, February 25). Expectations versus experiences of veterans with posttraumatic stress disorder (PTSD) service dogs: An inductive conventional content analysis. *Psychological Trauma: Theory, Research, Practice, and Policy, 14*(3), 347–56. http://dx.doi.org/10.1037/tra0001021

Nilsson, J., Hollandbeck, A., & Eustis, D. H. (2016, April). The Post article that launched the seeing eye program. *The Saturday Evening Post*. https://www.saturdayeveningpost.com/2016/04/post-article-launched-seeing-eye-program/

Nimer, J., & Lundahl, B. (2007). Animal-assisted therapy: A meta-analysis. *Anthrozoös, 20*(3), 225–38. https://doi.org/10.2752/089279307X224773

Odendaal, J. S. (2000). Animal-assisted therapy—magic or medicine? *Journal of Psychosomatic Research, 49*(4), 275–80. http://dx.doi.org/10.1016/S0022-3999(00)00183-5

Office of Fair Housing and Equal Opportunity. (2020). *Assessing a person's request to have an animal as a reasonable accommodation under the fair housing act (FHEO*

Notice FHEO-2020-01). US Housing and Urban Development. https://www.ani mallaw.info/sites/default/files/HUD%20FHEO%20Assistance%20Animals%20 Notice%202020.pdf

O'Haire, M. E. (2013). Animal-assisted intervention for autism spectrum disorder: A systematic literature review. *Journal of Autism and Developmental Disorders, 43*(7), 1606–22. https://doi.org/10.1007/s10803-012-1707-5

Papalia, A. O. (2018). Service dogs in schools: Legal, access, and educational issues. *Pennsylvania Teacher Educator, 17*(1), 1–9.

Parenti, L., Foreman, A., Meade, J., & Wirth, O. (2013). A revised taxonomy of assistance animals. *Journal of Rehabilitation Research and Development, 50*(6), 745–56.

Parenti, L., Wilson, N., Foreman, A. M., Wirth, O., & Meade, B. J. (2015, Summer). Selecting quality service dogs: Part 1: Morphological and health consideration. *APDT Chronicle of the Dog,* 71–77.

Pet Partners. (2021, July 7). *Changing the world through AAI: The history of Pet Partners.* https://petpartners.org/blog/changing-the-world-through-aai-the-history-of-pet -partners/

Peterson, L. (2003). *A little horse sense: One family's innovative approach to helping the blind.* The Guide Horse Foundation. http://guide-horse.org/art_biography_mag .htm

Pierce, K. L. (2018). *Understanding and working with service dog handlers.* Counseling Today. https://ct.counseling.org/2018/10/understanding-and-working-with-ser vice-dog-handlers/

Powell, D. R., Son, S. H., File, N., & San Juan, R. R. (2010). Parent–school relationships and children's academic and social outcomes in public school prekindergarten. *Journal of School Psychology, 48*(4), 269–92. https://doi.org/10.1016 /j.jsp.2010.03.002

Psychiatric Service Dog Partners. (2020, February 2). "Don't play service dog police" graphic. https://www.psychdogpartners.org/board-of-directors/board-activities/ advocacy

Public Health. (2020). Understanding how to accommodate service animals in healthcare facilities. https://www.phe.gov/Preparedness/planning/abc/Pages/service-ani mals.aspx

Ramp. J. (2020, February 6). Service animals in the lab: Who decides? NPR. https:// www.npr.org/2020/01/29/800911230/service-animals-in-the-lab-who-decides

Reid, D. K., & Weatherly Valle, J. (2004). The discursive practice of learning disability: Implications for instruction and parent–school relations. *Journal of Learning Disabilities, 37*(6), 466–81. http://dx.doi.org/10.1177/00222194040370060101

Reisen, J. (2018, January 29). *Working dogs doing jobs only dogs can do.* American Kennel Club. https://www.akc.org/expert-advice/lifestyle/working-dogs-jobs-dogs-can/

———. (2021, February 24). *Service dogs, working dogs, therapy dogs, emotional support dogs: What's the difference.* American Kennel Club. https://www.akc.org/ expert-advice/training/service-working-therapy-emotional-support-dogs/

Riveto, H. (2002). History and animal studies. *Society & Animals, 10*(4), 403–6. https://www.animalsandsociety.org/wp-content/uploads/2015/11/ritvo.pdf

Rothstein, L. (2018). Puppies, ponies, pigs, and parrots: Policies, practices, and procedures in pubs, pads, planes, and professions: Where we live, work, and play, and how we get there: Animal accommodations in public places, housing employment, and transportation, *Animal, 24*, 13. https://scholar.google.com/scholar?hl=en&as_sdt=0%2C44&q=Puppies%2C+Ponies%2C+Pigs%2C+and+Parrots&btnG=#d=gs_cit&u=%2Fscholar%3Fq%3Dinfo%3AhzRzrasH_vgJ%3Ascholar.google.com%2F%26output%3Dcite%26scirp%3D0%26hl%3Den

Rowley v. Board of Education of the Hendrick Hudson School District, 483 F. Supp. 528 (S.D.N.Y. 1980), 632 F.2d 945 (2nd Cir. 1982).

Schoenfeld-Tacher, R., Hellyer, H., Cheung, L., & Kogan, L. (2017). Public perceptions of service dogs, emotional support dogs, and therapy dogs. *International Journal of Environmental Research and Public Health, 14*(6), 642. https://doi.org/10.3390/ijerph14060642

Serpell, J. A. (2015). The human-animal bond. In L. Kalof (Ed.), *The Oxford Handbook of Animal Studies*. Oxford Handbooks Online. https://doi.org/10.1093/oxfordhb/9780199927142.013.31

Service Dog Central. (2020, March 6). *Access disputes*. https://servicedogcentral.org/content/access-disputes

Spruin, E., Mozova, K., Franz, A., Mitchell, S., Fernandez, A., Dempster, T., & Holt, N. (2019). The use of therapy dogs to support court users in the waiting room. *International Criminal Justice Review, 29*(3), 284–303. https://doi.org/10.1177/1057567719827063

Stafford, Robert T. 1978. Education for the handicapped: A senator's perspective. *Vermont Law Review, 3*, 71–76.

Tedeschi, P., Pearson, J. A., Bayly, D., & Fine, A. H. (2015). On call 24/7—The emerging roles of service and support animals. In A. Fine (Ed.), *Handbook on animal-assisted therapy* (4th ed., pp. 321–32). San Diego: Elsevier Academic Press.

The Dog Training Secret. (n.d.). *Why I said that dog should not be a service dog* [Blog post]. https://thedogtrainingsecret.com/blog/dog-should-not-be-service-dog/

The Seeing Eye. (n.d.). *History*. https://www.seeingeye.org/about-us/history.html

Therapy Dogs International. (n.d.). *Mission statement and history*. https://tdi-dog.org/About.aspx?Page=Mission+Statement+and+History

Tischler, J. (2008). The history of animal law, part I (1972–1987). *Stanford Journal of Animal Law & Policy, 1*, 1–49.

Trammell, J. P. (2017). The effect of therapy dogs on exam stress and memory. *Anthrozoös, 30*(4), 607–21. https://doi.org/10.1080/08927936.2017.13702

Traveller.com. (2020). *What is a service animal?* https://www.traveller.com.au/no-more-miniature-horses-us-limit-service-animals-on-planes-to-trained-dogs-h1l8sz

US Department of Health and Human Services, (2021). *Understanding how to accommodate service animals in healthcare facilities.* https://www.phe.gov/Preparedness/planning/abc/Pages/service-animals.aspx

US Department of Health, Education, and Welfare, Office for Civil Rights. (1978). *Section 504 of the Rehabilitation Act of 1973 Fact Sheet: Handicapped persons rights under federal law.* Washington, DC: Department of Health, Education, and Welfare, Office of the Secretary, Office for Civil Rights.

US Department of Justice. (2011, July). *ADA 2010 revised requirement: Service animals.* Civil Rights Division, Disability Rights Section. https://www.ada.gov/service_animals_2010.pdf

———. (2010). *Frequently asked questions.* https://www.ada.gov/service_animals_2010.htm

———. (2015). *Service animals.* https://www.ada.gov/service_animals_2010.htm

US Service Animals. (n.d.). *Miniature horses as service animals: What can they do?* [Blog post]. https://usserviceanimals.org/blog/miniature-horses-as-service-animals/

Wahl, J. M., Herbst, S. M., Clark, L. A., Tsai, K. L., & Murphey, K. E. (2008). A review of hereditary diseases of the German shepherd dog. *Journal of Veterinary Behavior: Clinical Applications and Research, 3*(6), 255–65. https://doi.org/10.1016/j.jveb.2008.05.004

Walther, S., Yamamoto, M., Thigpen, A. P., Garcia, A., Willits, N. H., & Hart, L. A. (2017). Assistance dogs: Historic patterns and roles of dogs placed by ADI or IGDF accredited facilities and by non-accredited U.S. facilities. *Frontiers in Veterinary Science, 4*, 1–14. https://www.frontiersin.org/article/10.3389/fvets.2017.00001

Wisch, R. F. (2021). *Table of state service animal laws.* Michigan State University Animal Legal & Historical Center. https://www.animallaw.info/topic/table-state-assistance-animal-laws

Yell, M. P., & Bateman, D. F. (2020). *Endrew F. v. Douglas County School District* (2017): Free appropriate public education and the U.S. Supreme Court, an update. *Teaching Exceptional Children, 52*(5), 283–90.

Young, R. L. (2013). Regarding Rocky: A theoretical and ethnographic exploration of interspecies intersubjectivity. *Society & Animals, 21*(3), 294–313. http://dx.doi.org/10.1163/15685306-12341272

Younggren, J. N., Boisvert, J. A., & Boness, C. L. (2016). Examining emotional support animals and role conflicts in professional psychology. *Professional Psychology, Research and Practice, 47*(4), 255–60. http://doi.org/10.1037/pro0000083

Zamir, T. (2006). The moral basis of animal-assisted therapy. *Society & Animals, 14*(2), 179–99. https://doi.org/10.1163/156853006776778770

INDEX

AAA. *See* animal-assisted activities
AAT. *See* animal-assisted therapy
ACA. *See* Air Carrier Access Act
ADA. *See* Americans with Disabilities Act
ADA National Network, 13
administrators
   policy considerations on service animal lack of control for, 96
   service animal prior experience of, 97
   service animals and, 3–4
Air Carrier Access Act (ACA), emotional support animals and, 27, 30, 32, 34–36
AKC. *See* American Kennel Club
AKC Canine Good Citizen's Test, ten performance tests of, 103, 111–12, *114–15*
alert dogs, 109–10
   autism use of, 57
   postsecondary education transition planning and, 140
   Rohena and Bright scenario of, 55, 65–66
   as service animals, 30
allergies, 40, 61–62, 73, 127, 129, 151–52
American Kennel Club (AKC), 111
Americans with Disabilities Act (ADA), 3, 7, 8, 11, 27, 86
   behavioral standards and access rights and FAPE in, 146–47
   as civil rights law, 70, 74, 125
   different tasks performance examples of, 39
   disability definitions of, 18, 33–34, 38, 120–21
   dual protection of, 69
   eligibility under, 70
   equal access guarantee of, 59–60, 64, 72, 87, 89, 124–25
   evaluation measures in, 71
   Fry v. Napoleon Community Schools and, 60–61
   invisible disability and, 118
   miniature horses separate provision of, 18, 56
   psychiatric service animals and, 32
   reasonable accommodations provision of, 72
   school requirements and, 71
   school visitors and, 59
   service animal definition of, 15, 32–33, 36, 58, 121, 123–24
   service dog and miniature horse recognition of, 56
   service dog identification difficulty under, 63–64
   student discrimination protection under, 59–60, 150
   therapy animals and, 30
   Title II service animal definition and care in, 20, 145–46, 147–48
   Title I on employment discrimination in, 136
   transition services and, 132–33
   violation knowledge concerning, 125
animal-assisted activities (AAA), 9
animal-assisted therapy (AAT), recognition of, 9–10
animal protection legislation, *Pierson v. Post* ruling on, 8
animal relief, 94, 98–99, 127–28
animals, fear of, 61–62, 73, 127, 129, 151–52

INDEX

assistance animals, 27, *31*
   ADA and, 32–33
   characteristics of, *28*
   dual-role, 35
   emotional support animals as, 32
   human-animal interaction benefits in, 28
   pets and, 28
   therapy animals as, 30–32
Assistance Dog International, 50
autism, 10, 30, 35, 38, 70
   alert dog use for, 57
   Jonas and Jinx scenario on, 55, 66–67, 143–44

Bateman, D. F., 149
Bergin, Bonnie, dog training of, 7
Burleson, Janet, miniature horses training of, 7–8

Canine Good Citizen (CGC) Test, 111–12
Child Find, 147
civil rights law, 70, 72, 74, 125
Cline, J. L., 149
control commands, 125–26
Corson, Elizabeth, 9
Corson, Samuel, "pet-facilitated psychotherapy" of, 9

Davidson and Radar scenario, 54, 65
Delta Society, Pet Partners program of, 9
Department of Education, 60
Department of Housing and Urban Development, 34
Department of Justice, US, 11, 60
   allergies or fear of dogs response of, 127
   emotional support animals and, 85
   service animal and emotional support and psychiatric service animals distinction of, 146
   Title II and, 20
Department of Transportation, US, 34, 58

dog as service animals, issues addressing of
   AKC Canine Good Citizen's Test use in, 103, 111–12, *114–15*
   basic obedience skills mastering for, 105–6
   behavioral and temperamental characteristics understanding in, 104
   behavioral assessment documentation for, 111
   behavioral criteria lack and, 107
   behavior drift and, 108
   consistent mistake and retraining in, 107
   dog and miniature horse species-specific implications in, 112–13
   error impact evaluation for, 104
   expectation defining in, 110, 113
   handlers and behavior reinforcement for, 108
   health issues and, 106
   home and public greeting criteria for, 107–8
   major issues framework for, 110–12
   minor error recognition for, 108–9
   nonaggression response training for, 105
   occasional mistake handling in, 107, 113
   out of control as major issue in, 109, 113
   perfectionism and unreasonable expectations in, 106
   performance ability assessment for, 111
   proactive problem-solving approach to, 105
   Public Access Test and, 103, 112
   release words use in, 108
   remediation action plan development for, 111
   remediation issues guidelines in, 104
   required task or alert behavior for, 109–10
   school reintegration and, 112

INDEX

service animal breakdown in, 103
service dog qualities in, 105
service handler skills assessment in, 111
trainer use in, 108
training program release reasons in, 104–5
uncontrolled behavior source identification in, 110
dogs, as service animals, 29
   access questions about, 3
   ADA and, 32, 56, 63–64
   administrators and, 3–4
   alert dogs as, 30
   ancient works of art regarding, 6
   characteristics of, 16, *28*
   children with autism use of, 10
   children with disabilities and, 3
   creative uses of, 10
   Europe beginning of, 6–7
   Eustis and training of, 7
   evolution of, 5–6
   handler relationship with, 6
   hearing and guide, 16–17
   human-animal bond research on, 8–9
   human use of, 5, 152
   increased usage of, 2, 143
   independence assisting of, 17
   Jonas and Jinx scenario of, 55, 66–67, 143–44
   law and housing of, 137
   learn from, 5
   legal and educational components of, 1–2
   legal definition of, 2
   local ordinances about training of, 33
   parent letter sample for, 102
   positive impact of, 10
   public places encountering of, 27
   school personnel access determination of, 1
   schools and, 1, 54–55
   school use guide for, 1
   as self-advocacy barrier, 118, 120
   specific training of, 2–3
   stakeholders and, 2
   students and, 4
   task determination and, 30
   training of, 17
   transition planning and, 4
   two legal questions about, 32–33, 35, 147
   vocabulary and titles importance in, 56
   World War I and II use of, 6
dogs as service animals, employment transition planning for, 4, 80, 141–42
   ADA and Section 504 regarding, 132
   ADA and Title I on employment discrimination in, 136
   ADA only coverage and, 132–33
   advance organizer for, 131
   animal-specific issues in, 133–34
   disability awareness component and example in, 134–35
   ecological analysis need and purpose in, 133–34
   elderly people handling skills and, 135
   employee and employer responsibility in, 136
   environmental and personal and service dog factors consideration in, 133
   incorporation in daily activities for, 131
   job functions and service animal relationship examination for, 135–36
   legal knowledge and access rights regarding travel and, 137
   McDonald v. Department of Environmental Quality case and, 136–37
   multiple settings examination for, 134
   new employment or educational environment demands in, 132
   new physical or task-related challenges for, 134
   public transportation distinctions in, 135

INDEX

reasonable accommodation and examples in, 136
service animal law and application knowledge for, 136
service animal work environment needs in, 135
service dog law and housing in, 137
special education and IDEA in, 132–33
strategic handling skills determination in, 134
transition services and student legal coverage in, 132
dogs as service animals, postsecondary education transition planning for, 4, 94, 142
accommodation and documentation in, 139
alert dogs and, 140
on campus living considerations for, 139
challenges in, 138
classroom arrangements consideration for, 140–41
class schedules and nature of class in, 140
environmental and personal and service dog factors considerations in, 138
high school to college transition in, 137
IDEA and ADA in, 139
invisible disabilities and service animal legitimacy in, 141
Office of Disabilities Services notifications in, 139
professor advance notification and service animal etiquette in, 140
reaction preparation for, 141
roommate considerations for, 140
self-advocacy skills development for, 141
service animal benefits and advantages in, 138
service animal play and relaxation time in, 140

social engagements and service animal in, 138
veterinary care and supplies consideration for, 138
"dry run," 99
dual protection, service animals and students with disabilities and special education, 59–61
direct threat addressing in, 73
educational responsibilities and, 70–71
evaluation components in, 71
guidelines for, 72–73
IDEA and ADA and Section 504 eligibility for, 69
law purposes in, 69–70
laws comparison impacting schools and service animals for, 74
laws eligibility differences in, 70
placement treatment in, 71–72
due process, 60–61, 149–50

Education for All Handicapped Children Act, 75
emotional support animals (ESA), 2, 18, 25, 45
characteristics of, 28
definition of, 14, 32
different roles of, 14
FHA and ACA legal protections of, 27, 32, 34–36
increased usage of, 143
Ming Lee and Elsie scenario for, 54, 65
pet differences with, 14
psychiatric service animals and, 57
reasonable accommodations for, 85
school access and, 58
service animal difference of, 15, 146
equal access, 59–60, 64, 72, 87, 89, 124–25
ESA. *See* emotional support animals
Eustis, Dorothy, 7
Ewoldt, Kathy B., 91

INDEX

Fair Housing Act (FHA), 27, 32, 35–36
  animal types protected by, 34
  emotional support animals and, 58
  therapy animals protection of, 30
  updated regulations of, 34
FAPE. *See* free appropriate public education
FHA. *See* Fair Housing Act
Frank, Morris, request letter of, 7
free appropriate public education (FAPE), 59, 86–87, 150
  ADA and, 146–47
  administrative hearing and, 88–89
  Fry v. Napoleon Community Schools and, 60–61
  as IDEA cornerstone, 23, 86
  OCR and, 22–23
  school districts obligation on, 72, 84–85, 145
  Section 504 requirements for, 22
  team service animal determination of, 23
Fry, Elhena, 60
Fry v. Napoleon Community Schools, 60–61, 67, 88–89, 150

Glenn, Margaret K., 131
Guide Horse Foundation, 8

handlers, 1–2, 47n1, 108, 111, 150
  common statements in schools to, 53
  as disabled person, 58
  Jonas and Jinx scenario regarding, 151
  Public Access Test ability assessment of, 103, 112
  public issues of, 118–19
  schools access and, 1, 53–55, 59
  service animal care of, 148, 152
  service animal control of, 12, 21, 35, 100, 146
  service animal relationship with, 6, 127
  tether use of, 12, 21, *100*, 146
  therapy animals and, 30–32, 57–58
  training participation of, 47
  unwanted attention danger of, 118–19, 122
Hartness, Kristin, 69
Human Methods of Livestock Slaughter Act, 8

IAADP. *See* International Association of Assistance Dog Partners
IDEA. *See* Individuals with Disabilities Act
Individualized Education Program (IEP), 3, 4
  accommodations or modifications and questions in, 79
  annual goals and questions in, 79
  annual progress and, 81–82
  behavioral intervention plan and, 80
  current assessment results and classroom performance questions for, 78–79
  development and implementation suggestions for, 82
  district service animal exclusion and, 86
  Education for All Handicapped Children Act and, 75
  expected progress factors in, 81
  FAPE administrative hearings and, 88–89
  Fry v. Napoleon Community Schools and, 60
  goal development or modification in, 82
  goal repetition and, 82
  IDEA and Section 504 significant differences and, 75–76
  IDEA implementation requirements and legal counsel recommendations in, 86–88
  key elements of, 84
  multidisciplinary team development of, 76–77
  needs addressing in, 85

parent copy of, 82
parents and teachers in, 77
PLAAFP statements as foundation of, 81
placement decision and, 83–84
placement questions in, 79–80
PLOPs and PLAFs and PLAAFP terms in, 77
progress phases in, 81
report summary questions in, 79
school districts obligation in, 84–85, 145
service animal back-up plan and, 148
service animal nondiscrimination and, 88
service animals and, 59, 64, 66–67, 85–86
special education assessment questions and, 78
special education student eligibility for, 76
specific program identification in, 78
state codes and, 88
student needs statement and addressing in, 77, 149
team meeting central concepts in, 83
three distinct phases of, 86
transition plan and, 80
transition services included in, 133
unique needs of student in, 82–84
as useful document, 83
Individuals with Disabilities Act (IDEA), 3, 11, 59
ADA and, 97, 139
Child Find component of, 147
comprehensive multidisciplinary evaluation in, 71
disability categories of, 70
dual protection of, 69
as education act, 70
eligibility under, 70
FAPE as cornerstone of, 23, 86
federal financial assistance of, 70
Fry v. Napoleon Community Schools and, 60–61
IEP regarding, 76
implementation requirements and legal counsel recommendations in, 86–88
placement decision in, 71
schools special education responsibility and, 70–71
Section 504 significant differences between, 75–76
service animal addressing of, 145
special education in, 132–33
transition services definition of, 133
International Association of Assistance Dog Partners (IAADP), 112
invisible disability
ADA and, 118
psychiatric service animals task knowledge of, 124
as self-advocacy skills barrier, 118–19, 121
service animal access and, 57
service animal legitimacy in, 141

Jonas and Jinx, 147
handler and animal and environment factors in, 151
questions to consider about, 143–44
scenario on, 55
solution to, 66–67

Kassem, Suzy, 5
Kuzma, Cindy, 37

least restrictive environment, 71, 74, 79, 83–84, 89
legal, educational, access, and strategic handling (LEASH), 143–44, 152
Levinson, Boris, 8–9

Marine Mammal Protection Act, 8
McDonald v. Department of Environmental Quality, 136–37

Mills, M., 121
Ming Lee and Elsie scenario, 54, 65
miniature horses as service animals, 1, 112–13
   ADA separate provision about, 18, 56
   allergies and, 40
   assessment factors for, 13, 18
   Burleson training of, 7–8
   cost-benefit ratio of, 19
   as exception to dog, 17
   federal regulations on, 12–13
   guide work of, 18
   life expectancy and, 19
   mobility disability aid of, 19, 30, 40
   Moses and Orient scenario for, 54
   Shaw and, 7–8
   three main benefits of, 29–30
   training requirements for, 19
Moses and Orient scenario, 54, 64

Office for Civil Rights (OCR), 22–23, 88

Papalia, Anne O., 1, 53
parents, 59, 77, 82, 97, 102
"pet-facilitated psychotherapy," 9
PLAAFP. *See* present levels of academic achievement and functional performance
placement
   dual protection in, 71–72
   IDEA and, 71
   IEP decision and questions about, 79–80, 83–84
   Section 504 and, 72
   service animal training after, 49
PLAFs. *See* present levels of academic function
play and relaxation time, 50, 140
PLOPs. *See* present levels of performance
post-traumatic stress disorder (PTSD), 30, 38–39, 50, 60, 86, 146
   Davidson and Radar scenario about, 54, 65

present levels of academic achievement and functional performance (PLAAFP), 77
present levels of academic function (PLAFs), 77
present levels of performance (PLOPs), 77
psychiatric service animals, 17, 25, 30
   ACA and, 35
   ADA and, 32
   characteristics of, *28*
   Davidson and Radar scenario regarding, 54
   Department of Justice distinction of, 146
   ESA and, 57
   invisible disabilities task knowledge for, 124
   as service animal, 15
   state law and, 124
   tasks of, 15–16, 85–86
Psychiatric Service Dog Partners, 117
PTSD. *See* post-traumatic stress disorder
public, 27, 107–8, 126, 129
   handlers issues with, 118–19
   service animal interest and behavior of, 98
   service animal law misunderstanding of, 118
   support dog familiarity of, 121
Public Access Test, dog and handler ability assessment in, 103, 112

reasonable accommodations, 24, 72, 85, 136
Rehabilitation Act, Section 504 of, 3, 11, 86
   as civil rights law, 70, 72, 74
   dual protection of, 69
   eligibility under, 70
   evaluation component in, 71
   FAPE requirements in, 22
   IDEA significant differences between, 75–76

IEP regarding, 76
important points on, 22
major life activities description of, 70
as nondiscrimination law, 21–22, 150
OCR and, 22–23
placement and, 72
school education under, 71
self-advocacy and, 124
service animal addressing of, 145–46
students with disabilities access and, 59
transition services and, 132
Reisen, Jan, on dogs, 27
Rohena and Bright scenario, 55, 65–66
Rosemary and Solomon scenario, 55, 66

school districts, 72, 84–86, 92, 101, 145, 148
schools, 11
 accommodation example for, 148
 assistance animals in, 27–35
 Child Find issue and, 147
 as community gathering place, 54
 Department of Justice and Title II regarding, 20
 due process complaints conditions in, 149–50
 employees with service animals regulations at, 24
 handler statements in, 53
 ineligibility and child evaluation in, 147
 legal obligation of, 149
 observational data and unmet needs assessment of, 149
 "qualified individual" and "reasonable accommodation" terms and, 24
 scenario answer factors for, 55
 service animal removal and, 20–21
 service animal task list and, 14
 service dog and handler access determination by, 1, 54
 service dog and handler access scenarios for, 54–55
 special education and due process hearing in, 150
 strategic handling factors for, 55–56
 student service animal control in, 21
 undue hardship factors for, 25
schools, service animal access in
 ADA definition determination for, 56
 alert dog types and, 57
 court criteria for, 56
 Davidson and Radar scenario and solution in, 54, 65
 emotional support animals and, 58
 Fry v. Napoleon Community Schools case
  about, 60–61, 150
 handler's role and nature of visit in, 59
 inquires limited nature in, 57
 invisible disability and, 57
 Jonas and Jinx scenario and solution and questions in, 55, 66–67, 143–44
 Ming Lee and Elsie scenario and solution in, 54, 65
 Moses and Orient scenario and solution in, 54, 64
 parents and guardians concerning, 59
 psychiatric service dogs and, 57
 Rohena and Bright scenario and solution in, 55, 65–66
 Rosemary and Solomon scenario and solution in, 55, 66
 service animals in training and, 58–59
 specific types of questions for, 57, 147
 strategic handling skills for, 61–64
 students with disabilities and, 59
 therapy animal and handler team in, 57–58
 three-step framework for, 56–61
 visitors with disabilities and, 59
schools, service animals in
 ADA and IDEA protection of, 97
 administration office purpose in, 92–93
 administration rights education in, 98
 administrators policy considerations on lack of control in, 96

INDEX

administrators prior experience in, 97
animal and crowded situations training for, 99
animal cleaning and grooming regularity and, 99
animal relief area for, 94
behavior and cleanliness of, 101
behavior protocols establishing for, 95
central administration considerations for, 93
children preparedness for, 95–96
as classroom experience, 91
daily navigation discussion for, 99
definitions and inquiries about, 100
district or building policy considerations in, 92
district registration and family notification in, 101
"dry run" for, 99
early notification of, 97
grievance handling for, 101
handler control and, 100
local identity protection regulations in, 94
logistical considerations and discussion for, 92, 98
master location schedule for, 93
parent collaboration in, 97
predictable routines and emergency procedures discussion in, 99
public interest and behavior dealing with, 98
registration and training in, 100
relief concern regarding, 98–99
resistance mitigation in, 96–97
school users full communication on, 93–94
service dog letter to parents sample for, 102
state and local requirements for, 100
student and teacher education in, 98
student behavior do's and don'ts for, 96
students and staff education in, 94–95

training frequency and depth in, 95
transition handling of, 94
two legal questions for, 92, 147
waste removal frequency in, 94
Section 504. *See* Rehabilitation Act, Section 504 of
self-advocacy skills, barriers to
access issues misunderstanding in, 119
animal fraudulent representation increase in, 121
development of, 118
disability definition misunderstanding and, 120–21
dog breeds and, 119–20
fake service animals and handler experiences with, 118
federal and state service animal laws misinterpretation in, 119
handler public issues and, 118–19
handlers and unwanted attention danger in, 122
identification requirements in, 121–22
inappropriate behavior tasks in, 123
invisible disability confrontation in, 118–19, 121
legal ambiguity and, 121
pet policy norm in, 119
public's misunderstanding of service animal law and, 118
public support dog familiarity in, 121
purposeful disobedience and, 123
service animals and quality of life in, 117–18, 128
service animal tasks and dog sizes in, 120
service dog etiquette in, 118
service dog legitimacy and, 120–21
specialized equipment use in, 120
standardized certification lack in, 121–22
stereotypical views about animal appearance for, 120

unwanted attention consequences in, 122–23
self-advocacy techniques, 141
  ADA and Section 504 practical application in, 124
  ADA violation knowledge as, 125
  allergies or fear of dogs addressing in, 127, 129
  animal energy and time protection for, 128, 129
  attitude as key component in, 125
  compromise areas identification in, 127
  equal access and, 124–25
  essential control commands use in, 125–26
  law and tasks statements for, 128
  legal knowledge sharing of, 124, 128
  major elements of, 123
  other animal awareness as, 128
  physical space needs in, 126
  public interactions difficulty in, 126, 129
  relief breaks and potential hazards handling in, 127–28
  scenario practice in, 127
  service animal and equal access distinction in, 125
  service animal and handler relationship in, 127
  service animal etiquette examples and materials use for, 126, 129
  service animal federal definition for, 123–24
  service animal's abilities and needs recognition in, 127
  state and local law knowledge in, 124
  statement of rights example for, 129
  strategic handling skills practice for, 125
  task-related information sharing for, 124
service animal etiquette, 62, 118, 126, 129, 140, 151
service animal legitimacy, 120–21, 141
service animals, federal regulations related to
  definition and exceptions to, 11–12
  Department of Justice, US, and, 11
  on handler's control, 12
  individual's disability work or tasks examples in, 13–14
  miniature horses and, 12–13
service animals, training and acquisition, 2–3, 17, 58–59, 95, 99–100
  accredited organization use in, 50–51
  actual cost of, 45
  agency training questions for, 42
  age requirement and, 47
  all day or intermittent work of, 49
  animal needs discussion in, 48–50
  animal playtime and relaxation in, 50
  annual costs of having, *41*
  calm and alert training for, 43
  care for, 39
  command ability for, 47–48
  different tasks performance of, 39
  disability and reasons for, 38
  disability severity and, 38
  dog temperament addressing in, 40
  financial assistance organizations for, 42, 45, 51
  financial investments in, 38
  follow-up need in, 42
  handler or person with disability in, 47
  handler participation in, 47
  individual need focus in, 44
  information transfer in, 44
  "in house" training and, 43
  intermittent reinforcement in, 44
  local ordinances about, 33
  long-term ramifications in, 37–38
  long-term support importance in, 47
  miniature horses and, 7–8, 19, 40
  need dictates type in, 39–40
  other animals and problems in, 40, 48
  parent genetics and history in, 46

INDEX

personal and disability-related factors considerations in, 38
positives and negatives addressing for, 41
provider choosing for, 45–46
regulations and, 45
repetitive tasks ability in, 44
requalification requirements for, 48–49
requirements for, 44–45
respect and dignity in, 48
rest importance in, 50
roles and responsibilities understanding in, 47
socialization and specific tasks training in, 43–44
space and housing in, 40
stable home environment and, 48
taxes and, 45
trainer questions for, 46
training after placement for, 49
training programs and costs for, 42
upkeep of, 41
Shaw, Dan, 7–8
Smith, Elaine, 9
special education, 70–71, 76, 78, 132–33, 150
See also dual protection, service animals and students with disabilities and special education
Stafford, Robert, 75
State Supreme Court of Montana, *McDonald v. Department of Environmental Quality* case and, 136–37
strategic handling skills, 55–56, 64, 134
compromise discussion in, 152
control as contextual in, 151
environmental factors and risk assessments in, 63
examples of, 61
fear of animals and allergies in, 61–62, 73, 151–52

handler and animal and environment interaction in, 150
Jonas and Jinx case involving, 151
proactive planning for student support in, 62
school notification as, 61
self-advocacy techniques for, 125
service animal class visits in, 62
service animal injury in, 63
service animal law and etiquette training as, 62, 151
service animal responsibility in, 62
teachers and, 62
students, 62
ADA and, 59–60, 150
dual coverage and due process involving, 60–61
IEP for, 76–77, 82–84, 149
school district data use on, 145
school district responsibility for, 148
schools and, 94–95, 98
Section 504 access and, 59
service animal control of, 21
service animals and, 4
service animals do's and don'ts for, 96
special education and dual legal coverage of, 59–60
transition planning and, 4, 132
See also dual protection, service animals and students with disabilities and special education
Supreme Court, US
Endrew F. decision of, 78, 81
Fry v. Napoleon Community Schools case and decision of, 60–61, 67, 88–89, 150

TDI. *See* Therapy Dogs International
teachers, 62, 77, 98
therapy animals, 2, 9–10, *28*, 121–22
ACA and FHA protection of, 30
characteristics of, 31
increased usage of, 143

as individually trained pets, 31
Rosemary and Solomon scenario about, 55
school access and, 57–58
social and emotional support of, 30–31
social interaction training of, 30
training of, 32
Therapy Dog Alliance, 9
Therapy Dogs International (TDI), 9, 35, 55, 66
Truman, Harry S., 143, 152

www.ingramcontent.com/pod-product-compliance
Lightning Source LLC
Chambersburg PA
CBHW070806230426
43665CB00017B/2502